CLIMBING
THE CORPORATE
PYRAMID

CLIMBING
THE CORPORATE
PYRAMID

MARTIN R. MILLER

amacom

A DIVISION OF AMERICAN MANAGEMENT ASSOCIATION

International standard book number: 0-8144-5314-7
Library of Congress catalog card number: 72-86427

First printing

FOREWORD

How we interact with others becomes a measure of who we are. I would like to feel that this book, the result of a kaleidoscope of life experiences, can help people relate to others in a helpful and constructive way—both in and out of the business world.

To all my friends who labored, sweated, and strained with me on this project: thank you.

MARTIN R. MILLER

CONTENTS

GETTING IT ALL TOGETHER FOR SUCCESS 1

A top executive at the Radio Corporation of America was fond of telling his staff that a man's success in business depends on his ability to convince people that he has something they want. All business leaders know this, either consciously or unconsciously.

Many versions of this basic truth have been communicated by articulate men, but what is always implied is that one must first know what he has that makes him indispensable to people or to an organization. "Know thyself," first uttered by an ancient Greek sage, remains a prerequisite for anyone who craves success at whatever he undertakes—be it bricklaying or running General Motors.

Many low-level managers with high-level aspirations, however, cling to the myth that there are texts and formulas that enable "one of the boys" to reach the peak in a company. A large part of the myth centers on a mistaken conception of the learning process. Most education experts agree that a person does not become a leader by mastering a set of rules. There is a great difference between memorizing a formula and learning. The dependence on set patterns that stress rote studies really begins to manifest itself as a manager climbs in a company. After the first or second promotion, there are no rules, and the man who cannot conceptualize or who is thrown off balance by a new learning situation finds himself immobilized.

For despite mounds of management studies and psyche probes by behavioral scientists, top executive behavior in all its wonderful variety continues to elude pigeonhole classification. There is an old boardroom tale about the millionaire businessman whose marketing decisions always escalated company profits. He was respected and envied for his acumen until the day one of his lieutenants discovered that he never made a decision without first consulting an astrologer!

Beware the beast of certainty, for he reinforces rigidity and can cripple the growing executive. A large majority of industry seers, some self-proclaimed and others hired hands, tend to be dogmatic. After all, they are supposed to have all the answers, and are paid handsomely for them. In fact, some even admit that they are hired to make decisions that a company refuses to make itself. And if the "suggestions" do not work out, the consultee has a convenient scapegoat under contract.

Is There a Pattern for Success?

There is a myriad of books, studies, and "expert" opinions on how one achieves success. Some studies show that the absence of material comforts as a child spurs a man on to great success; others reveal that the advantaged child born of middle- or upper-class parents succeeds. But all the studies, all the high-toned pieces in the sophisticated business journals, and all the diverse opinions of management men only confirm that there is no one formula for success.

For every well-educated and culturally advantaged white Anglo-Saxon Protestant businessman who has become a corporate power, there are thousands of failures. And the lower class certainly manages to produce a fair share of corporate giants.

True, the ethnic outsider, through hard and frustrating experience in trying to crack the corporate boardrooms of the economy's cornerstone companies, has found the entrepreneurial route to wealth and its accompanying prestige easier and perhaps more satisfying. The entrepreneurial route, moreover, is often the only path available.

If you are looking for formulas or infallible prescriptions larded with supporting statistics for success—close this book. If you are searching for an easy guide with which to follow competitor get-ahead tactics—stop reading. However, if you are currently positioned a few steps up on the corporate pyramid—read on. If you are willing to take an introspective trip into your psyche—keep turning the pages.

If there is any one theme of this book it is this: Person-to-person competence is a major ingredient in the fuel that powers ambitious men into corporate hierarchies. A man with technical skills can make it if he combines a knowledge of behavior (and acts on that knowledge) with his particular expertise; a generalist *must* be interpersonally competent because that is usually his major area of operation. And a technician without sensitivity to himself and others is like a computer. He can be programmed, but he cannot lead,

3

and he will always be dependent on directions from others. He will continue to look for mechanical explanations of human behavior. To paraphrase Napoleon: Technique breeds only refinements of existing technique, but imagination rules the world.

Specialists Versus Generalists

Back in the 1950s, a few wise businessmen accurately predicted the 1960s trend to specialization. More importantly, these men foresaw the problems inherent in specialization.

Here is what the chairman of the board of International Harvester Company had to say way back in 1953:

> . . . the world of the specialist is a narrow one and it tends to produce narrow human beings. The specialist usually does not see over-all effects on the business and so he tends to judge good and evil, right and wrong, by the sole standard of his own specialty.
>
> This narrowness of view, this judgment of all events by the peculiar standards of his own specialty, is the curse of the specialist from the standpoint of top management consideration for advancement. Except in unusual cases, it tends to put a roadblock ahead of him after he reaches a certain level.*

Today, many top thinkers in the business world believe that the cycle of technicians is winding down and that more and more executives with liberal arts educations will bloom in the 1970s. Preliminary evidence bears this out. There are proportionately more liberal arts students than engineering or technically oriented students in our schools as the 1970s begin.

* *Fortune* (September 1953), p. 129.

4

Youngsters today are beginning to shy away from the technical professions, perhaps from the lesson learned from seeing many skilled men out of work because of a slowdown in the economy in 1970. The young executives who will become the top men during the 1970s are already serving notice on their elders that they will not be forced into a narrow slot on an organization chart that pays well, but that does not offer mobility or intellectual satisfaction.

The howls of outrage of most top management men echo through the boardrooms. "Those damned kids. What do they want? They are bright, but their attitude . . ." These executives feel challenged and are angry about being pushed to reexamine long held, rarely questioned values. These men would do well to harness the energy and life that the new-breed executive possesses. The new generation of Young Turks is just as eager to get ahead as any other generation.

Identifying Potential Leaders

The problem of predetermining potential leaders remains a guessing game: There is a plethora of studies in print on men already at the top, but only a sprinkling of work on future company presidents.

One of the most exhaustive studies ever made to determine whether or not young executives have top management potential was dubbed the Early Identification of Management Potential (EIMP). Developed by the Standard Oil Company of New Jersey over a period of six years prior to its adoption in 1961, the EIMP program was "based on the beliefs that there are individual differences between the more successful and less successful members of management, that these differences can be measured and that they can be measured early in the careers of employees, and that a successful candidate for a management position will have a better chance of being successful if his own characteristics are like those of the more successful managers.''

The program, now referred to as the Personnel Development Series, continues in use at Standard Oil and a number of its affiliates. The original study was significant for its attempt to predict potential ''for positions many levels above the individuals' present assignments.'' The original test group consisted of a final total of 443 managers at all stages of the company —from company officers and board members down to first and second level supervisors.

A battery of tests made up the bulk of the program, but one in particular is acknowledged by Standard Oil as the best of the ''predictors.'' The Individual Background Survey (IBS), a quasi personality test, ''measures such characteristics as independence, maturity, sociability, social responsibility, and certain kinds of vocational and avocational interests.'' The IBS developed for the program resembles an interview on paper.

A number of conclusions from the findings can serve as guidelines for managerial hopefuls. For example, managers in the higher positions tended to be older and have longer service in the company. Nothing new or unexpected in that finding. However, managers who were at the top level of the scale on managerial effectiveness, no matter where they were on the organization chart, were younger and had shorter service in the company.

Upper level managers were found to spend more time politicking and less time on the technical aspects of their jobs than did the lower level managers.

The higher up a manager was, the more education he had, but the intelligence tests indicated that the scores of the men in top positions were only slightly higher than those of the lower level managers. In addition, the high position managers were found to be more independent and aggressive than their lower level counterparts.

Two Major Ingredients for Success

Apparently most behavioral scientists agree that there are two major intangibles that the top executive usually possesses—drive, or aggressiveness, and independence. The first can derive from a variety of psychological antecedents; the second is born of experience and an inner sense of security.

Ask an acknowledged leader in any industry how he reached the top and the answer is inevitably much duller than the man. Most executives reply in cliches: "I worked hard." "I kept my eyes and ears open." "I was lucky, I guess." It's hard to believe, but some even say they don't know how they did it. Most successful men are not aware of how they differ from the men they have surpassed. Perhaps it is false modesty, but a pronounced humility creeps into the conversation when top achievers discuss their own success. I have interviewed a number of these men and the only time they seem to talk in abstractions is when they discuss their own reasons for doing well in business.

But even in the laconic statement "I worked hard" one can see the emphasis on drive, a word that drops with notable frequency from the lips of top executives. This is particularly true when they discuss the qualities they look for in managerial "comers." Cynics may say that a carhop has drive, but there is a difference between nervous energy and competitive striving.

But if one were to search for a modern version of the

7

Horatio Alger story he might look outside the business world—to the driving example of the late Vince Lombardi, the greatly respected professional football coach. Lombardi succeeded from every angle of corporate perception. Here was a man who came from what is sometimes referred to as a "humble beginning." Here was a man who pushed himself to the limits of what he could achieve. He had all the attributes necessary for success in the American business system. Although not large physically (he weighed only about 175 pounds when he became known as one of the Seven Blocks of Granite on a late 1930s Fordham team), he managed to become one of the best linemen in the country. Not afraid to assess his own talents realistically, he refused, while an assistant coach for the New York Giants, a number of offers to become an assistant coach for a rival team. He finally accepted a job as head coach of the proud, but at the time unsuccessful, Green Bay Packers. Even the marginal sports fan had to notice the man's rapid rise to the top of his profession.

Lombardi combined a clearheaded knowledge of his attributes with a knowledge of his goals. He pursued these goals with a fierce will and an uncommon dedication.

Is Business a Game?

Business has often been referred to as an aggressive corporate game frequently played out in cutthroat style, with the bodies of losers left strewn about the industrial wayside. Perhaps that is why the contact sport of professional football appeals to corporate climbers. True, a cross section of the American male population is enamored of the sport, but along Madison

Avenue's advertising row, there are numerous profiles of the TV football fan, and many of the studies show him to be a driver and a man on the way up in his firm.

Football's combination of highly complex alignments and maneuvers with simplicity of physical contact is deeply satisfying to the competitive instinct. Competition, competition. And at the end of each Sunday afternoon, there is a winner and a loser. It is almost like a cowboy and Indian shoot-'em-up—except that the viewer doesn't know the outcome in advance (a fact that adds an extra edge to the competitiveness).

To classify the corporate climb as a game is to put it into a context that is, at least on the surface, more obviously compatible with the essence of competition American style. By considering the struggle for corporate power and all its attendant benefits in terms of a game, the "player" feels he can then better rationalize his efforts—he can focus on strategy and tactics.

Yet this is a myth—because such a rationalization leaves out the interpersonal dynamics of "getting ahead." There has to be an interplay between people, not things. No one ever succeeds in the business world without having some self-knowledge and an understanding of others. The disease of personal myopia must be avoided. So, of course, must nearsightedness at a broader level. Harvard's noted marketing professor, Theodore Leavitt, coined the term "marketing myopia." In his now famous paper,* Leavitt discussed the railroad industry and explained how it slowly languished because it never faced its problems realistically. The railroad men were "railroad-oriented," not "transportation-oriented." According to Leavitt, they

* "Marketing Myopia," *Harvard Business Review* (July–August 1960).

thought they were still concerned with the product and not the customer. To take another familiar example: When Hollywood realized it was an entertainment industry and not a "movie" business, it could recover from the initial onslaught of television.

The Importance of Objectivity

Almost all the top executives I have known as a business writer and editor have been able to avoid personal myopia. They have cultivated the ability to objectify. They may be what sociologist David Riesman has termed "inner-directed" or "other-directed," but they share one attribute: the ability to analyze their life situation and tune it to what they want.

"Know thyself" is true enough, but if you know yourself, you also know something about others and can begin to anticipate patterns of behavior in certain situations. A top executive can problem-solve, but he usually does not have to because he has anticipated the problem and has "handled" it in advance. How many people have you heard say about a top man: "He never seems to be caught unawares by a situation"?

Anticipation plays a large part in achieving success. If you can anticipate what is going to happen in your company, you can almost calculate your chances for advancement. The succeeding chapters are not going to supply answers, because each corporate situation is unique, but they will be helpful if some of the variables discussed are present in your company.

If technical skills are most desired by small, family-held, or entrepreneurial enterprises, then the top men in large companies must be generalists with strong interpersonal abilities. Unfortunately, as an executive advances and grows older, his behavioral patterns become more rigid. Also, the learning process, so necessary for taking the next and hardest steps up the corporate ladder, diminishes.

The Role of Curiosity

Studies on what companies look for and expect in new managers grow like crabgrass and are about as useful. Usually if one reads them in report form, he becomes convinced that any Boy Scout qualifies and could assume the helm of General Motors.

It is easy to list the attributes for success; it is another matter to live them. Living them begins at an early age, which is why top executives can be compared to children in many ways. I say that not pejoratively, but in a most complimentary way. For example, the child is curious; so is the top executive. How many times have you had the experience of talking to a person on an airplane without realizing that you were feeding him all kinds of information about yourself—your job, your home life, your aspirations? After leaving the plane, you realize that the man who was so curious about you was an astute leader and often a man in a position of power in his company.

One of the requisites for independence is curiosity. If a child is not curious to explore the world around him, then he is reluctant to move outside his own sphere and add the knowledge that would make him more independent.

The most successful men I know are still curious about almost everything. Like children, they have retained their inquisitiveness and have remained open to experience; this makes them better able to cope with business problems. As the proverb says, ''Experience is the teacher of us all.''

Nobody likes a loser in a competitive system. But

11

contrary to prevalent popular belief, there is no magical difference between the man who makes it and the man who doesn't. Most men in the business world fall somewhere between these extremes. Since we live in a competitive society which stresses the myth that the best man always wins, the first logical step to success is to clearly understand the system. That accomplished, the ambitious man can adjust his personality to fit.

Know Your Company

It is possible to study a corporation's personality patterns. People in a company reflect the company personality. Just as the child reflects the patterns and traits of those with whom he has the most contact, so people mirror the image of the corporation. The barefooted, miniskirted secretary at the reception desk of a high-powered advertising agency communicates a feeling about the company, just as a predominant number of aged executives says something about another company.

If you have been in a company a long time, however, it may be somewhat difficult to perceive objectively what the unspoken rules are. When you feel that you are too close to a situation, ask a perceptive, objective friend outside the company to help you see the company's true personality. What appears normal to a person in a work situation often seems abnormal to someone outside the firm.

Often there is a commonality of attitudes toward company problems that results in unspoken internal group pressures. For example, if, in a large midwestern company, all the top echelon leaders are members of the conservative wing of the Republican party, one could infer that they would favor right-to-work laws and oppose strong unions.

The company certainly would reflect the life style of its leaders. Such a firm might ban miniskirts, long hair, or even mustaches.

Tuning in to the company's individuality is as important as having all the other aptitudes and personal qualifications for success. Determining the true corporate personality includes piecing together elements of the following: (1) the life styles of key men, (2) the company's history (particularly if it is family run), (3) the policy trends, (4) the position of the company in its particular industry.

An Example of Corporate Personality

A good example of a company with a clearly defined personality is the Maytag Company, located in Newton, Iowa. The firm has a deserved reputation for producing a quality line of home laundry equipment. It is known as a "specialist." Loosely translated, this means that the company has evolved or managed to convey a rather steadfast, reliable image in an industry (the appliance business) that is not ordinarily noted for its conservative character. Over the years, Maytag has built up its dealerships and sold direct to them—thereby establishing a paternalistic, controlling pattern. Its leadership has come up through the ranks; very rarely has the company gone to outside companies for an infusion of new managerial blood. This means that the men who come to power in the company have had years of working and living in a small-town atmosphere, and have come to reflect the traditions of a one-company town.

Although the company has had to make concessions

in an industry that is noted for annual model changes and widespread price and product competition (for years the company resisted the standard industry practice of annual model changes), it has maintained its share of the market quite well. Of course, the company is an exception, but it is interesting to note that at one point in its history, Maytag decided to market a full line of kitchen appliances. By doing so the company could increase its overall sales, even though it would encounter stiffer competition from General Electric, Westinghouse, Frigidaire, and other "full line" companies. After a brief fling, the company abandoned the idea and reverted to its safe and tried formula for success. In this instance the idea of growth may have deviated too much from the company's set personality pattern to be tolerated.

What About Nonconformity?

A favorite question of young managers: "Will I be swallowed up in a larger organization—will my needs be ignored?" There are no definite answers because each organization's tolerance level for nonconformists varies. But one factor seems apparent: the higher up the scale you progress and the more skills you develop, the greater the chance your nonconformist tendencies will be tolerated. But acceptance is based on recognizable talent and skills. Sooner or later, the executive hopeful becomes aware of the paradox inherent in the corporate system. For, while the system encourages individuality in the higher echelons, it promotes conformity and keeps a tight rein on creativity on lower levels. It does so for a variety of reasons— mainly to keep a hand on the spigot that controls productivity.

Consider what this can mean: a man is promoted out

14

of the conformity-conscious lower echelon. He must now transform his ingrained pattern of conformity into an ongoing flexibility and creativity. If he has had his curiosity and drive successfully crushed at the lower work level, he will not be able to handle a new job or he will come into great conflict when he has to exhibit a growth orientation at a higher level.

The man is faced with the prospect of making decisions with greater consequence for his life and career than at any previous time. This paradox leads to the absolute wastage of many good men. If a man can survive in the lower echelons, the permanent scars may be too great when he reaches the upper levels and finds himself inadequately prepared. The atrophy encouraged on the lower level has succeeded; no amount of exercise can restore the creative muscles.

But there is still room for the individualist—if he is respected for prior achievements. It is another of the paradoxes of the American corporate system, which supposedly exalts the individual, that truly independent individuals who are innovators are given lip service and left to "other" companies to hire. Most companies look for the man who "fits in" and will "adjust" to the company. The nonconformist has a better chance with a small company that must do something original or offbeat to establish itself in a market that is usually dominated by older, well-established firms.

As the Standard Oil Company program (EIMP) indicated, the higher position manager shows more independence than those at lower levels. And almost by definition, independent men are nonconforming.

In fact some researchers say that the single biggest factor leading to management success is the unique way men respond to situations. After all, how a man adapts to a situation he finds himself in is not the same as the abdication of independent thought or behavior.

Some New Corporate Trends

The trend to tolerate nonconformists in the corporate structure should accelerate in the next decade because of two factors. One is the more flexible attitude of the leaders of tradition-breaking companies. These leaders are younger and not as tightly bound to rules as were their predecessors. The second is the rise of the conglomerate—which in many cases is managed by men under 45 years of age.

The multicompany makeup of the conglomerate enhances opportunity for the young man on the move. He has a choice of companies, all under the same banner, each with a different personality. In addition, the men at the top encourage rapid movement internally.

In the 1950s and 1960s the corporate comer in a large company could be spotted. He was the man who had handled a number of different assignments and been moved rather often in the corporate structure. In addition, he was still relatively young. The difference in this, the conglomerate era, is that there are more areas where a man can make an impression. Which leads directly to another area of top management capability. The manager must indeed be a man on the move. He must be willing and able to make rapid adjustments to new locations and assignments. If he fears new life situations and the creative contact it takes to cope with them, he will be reluctant to undertake any new movement that may challenge or upset a comfortable mold or style of living. The mobile executive who will eventually make the grade must

16

be tired of hearing the old refrain from his new neighbors and friends: "But how do you manage to move so much? Isn't it hard on you and your family?" This usually ends with a rationalization for nonmovement, usually put forth as: "No job promotion is worth all that." Variations might be: "But all my friends are here and my children are settled. Besides, my whole family lives in this area and it's where I grew up." The willingness to leave home, physically and mentally, is what distinguishes the independent man. Most top executives exhibit an independence based in large part on early mental separation from parental control.

Another quality necessary for upward mobility is the ability to function while feeling disorganized. Disorganization is inevitable for the rising management executive, usually afflicting him when he is in the process of learning something new. New learning displaces old patterns and forces him to discard prior notions. This process often results in a temporary state of confusion or disorganization until the experience is either integrated positively or rejected as too threatening to his self-image. It is a myth that the president of a company is never disorganized. Don't believe it. He may appear "put together" and in command at board meetings or department-level gatherings, but he has the same fears and questions as subordinates about courses of action and important decisions. He is not an all-knowing, imperturbable master of all situations. Speak to any candid wife of a company president and she will let slip a story of her husband's humanness and periods of "confusion." Most executives are comfortable in their roles only because they have had extensive experience in making decisions.

17

The Myth of Automatic Advancement

A final word about a persistent myth that everyone intellectually recognizes as a myth, but still believes in and clings to emotionally. No one who has decided to get ahead in a company can depend on being just an efficient producer. Ask any tired, old man after his brief moment of corporate glory at the annual retirement dinner. Yes, he produced. No, he did not advance very far in the company.

What many "strong team men" and "wonderful producers" realize too late in their careers, if at all, is that power is gathered by somehow neutralizing or outshining rivals. So, if you are on your way up the corporate pyramid, the struggle for power is going to become more and more intense.

What Harry Truman said of the Presidency might be applicable: "If you can't stand the heat, get out of the kitchen."

JOB STRESS: BOON OR BANE?

2

"At a crisis in my youth he taught me the wisdom of choice: to try and fail is at least to learn; to fail to try is to suffer the inestimable loss of what might have been."

That is the dedicatory quote to his father made by Chester I. Barnard in his classic study *The Functions of the Executive,* first published over 30 years ago and the precursor of numerous studies and theories on corporate organizations. The quote is highly applicable to a top executive in a stress situation.

This chapter is primarily devoted to helping you not become an also ran in the corporate sweepstakes. While it's not intended as a rationale for tension states, it does acknowledge that tension, or anxiety, exists in the very nature of man, who is free to use it or avoid it in all life situations. The focus here is on how it affects and is constructively used by executives. This chapter might well have been subtitled "The True Functions of Anxiety" or possibly "In Praise of Anxiety."

Anxiety Defined

Anxiety is a feeling that arises out of internal conflict and that occurs both in situations that are overtly stressful and in situations that do not appear so to the casual observer. It can lead to a proclivity "to fail to try." It may show itself in fretfulness over writing a memo, apprehension over making a presentation, trepidation over a new assignment. All these can call up a man's stubborn defense mechanisms, which have been built into and fortified in his personality over many years. Stress shrinks as the experience of trying increases, or as one clings more tenaciously to "comfortable" avoidance operations.

But first, let us try to define anxiety as it will be used in this chapter. Anxiety results from fear— fear of rational and realistic conditions on the one hand, or fear that is the product of distorted or unrealistic perceptions nurtured over many years. The man who can differentiate between anxiety called up by distorted perceptions, and anxiety based on a realistic appraisal of a threat to his survival, is better able to take the step that would lead to personal growth patterns. Anxiety is a signal that you are entering forbidden territory, and is the result of reinforced past experiences of fear, dread, or apprehensiveness about action. Overcoming an unrealistic predisposition to anxiety involves taking a chance on life by shedding the accumulated layers of defenses adopted for the purpose of avoiding decisive personal action.

Once one is clear that this life tension is self-generated, that it does not come from a mysterious source not open to discussion, one is able to examine it more closely and channel it into more positive uses. One of the major stumbling blocks for executives is that eventually their irrational fears and their attendant anxiety levels escalate as they progress in the corporate structure. Some men are affected severely, others hardly at all. In the latter category are the men who are able to adjust to or overcome areas of tension. They foresee their own problems, quickly resolve them, and go on to top positions.

The Effects of Stress and Avoidance

It is no accident that a plethora of studies show that states of stress are more common in executives than in people not in top leadership positions. The catalog of executive illnesses is legendary—ulcers and hypertension are perhaps the two most common. It is also true that the higher up one manages to go, the less chance there is of succumbing to serious psychosomatic illnesses. But it is also true that the majority of illness occurs at the levels just before the top—where the competition is the keenest and the driving the hardest.

So the purpose of this chapter is not to suggest ways to avoid stress; stress is inevitable if one is to move ahead. As I have stated before, growth involves a large, but not paralyzing, dose of tension. But to move positively, one must correctly perceive obstacles in the path of preset goals. Once a man understands that tension is self-generated, he is better able to examine his style to see how he avoids doing what has to be done to further his self-promotion.

What is meant by avoidance? Obviously, all of us tend to avoid painful or unpleasant situations. The problem is that when the role of avoidance becomes a major factor in our lives, we shun facing real situations —positive and negative. When we do that, anxiety decreases, or at least submerges, but at the same time we do not move forward. So we buy security at the enormous price of personal growth. We feel "more comfortable."

There is the familiar example in which one puts off firing a man who obviously deserves to be fired. Instead of facing the reality of the situation, the executive tries to reform the man. Or he may ignore the situation completely and involve himself with details that have nothing to do with the problem at hand. Equivocation upsets the man who should be fired, and the other employees empathically sense a tension or anxiety that has been dissociated. The executive has bought temporary comfort, but the situation will surface again and he will be forced to deal with it. The top executive copes, the second-rater avoids with a series of stopgap measures. The doer acts on his conflicts. He is not committed to the dynamics of avoidance.

This type of person differs from the escapist, who does act, but almost always avoids what needs doing or refuses to examine a particular aspect of his behavior. The top executive, because he is less committed to a self-restrictive policy of avoidance, is willing to live with his fears and anxieties because the goal he sets for himself is greater than his need to adjust, to "get along," and to settle for being one of the lower echelon members in a corporate hierarchy. He has faced his fear of the unknown. He gives up old ideas, replaces them with new ones, and learns from the anxiety that results from change.

Probably the most common example occurs when an executive moves to a higher level. The tensions that result from coping with a new situation become less of a factor if one just plunges ahead while maintaining flexibility.

Consider the Less-Traveled Road

Many junior executives "plateau out" because they do not want to cope with the anxieties involved in dealing with a person who represents the system (authority). They avoid the responsibility for the movement necessary to satisfy awakened inner needs.

It is a little like Robert Frost's poem "The Road Not Taken." In the poem, Frost comes upon two roads. He decides to take the one that "was grassy and wanted wear." Once on the road he "doubted if I should ever come back." At the end of the poem Frost notes:

Somewhere ages and ages hence:
Two roads diverged in a wood, and I—
I took the one less travelled by,
And that has made all the difference.

A man has been traveling down his life path. As he moves along he becomes more comfortable and is able to notice more. He sees that one road ahead is different, the other is a continuation of the same road he has been traveling. Which should he take? Most men would take the well-traveled path, even at the expense of passing up a challenge. So it is within a company. The well-worn road is crowded with men who have reached their self-imposed limits. The other road may be rocky at times but it is not as crowded and does offer challenges.

If you decide to take a less traveled route to the top in your chosen corporation, remember that upward movement can be a disruptive experience for individuals not attuned to the social milieu they enter. Numerous studies show that the rough-hewn production man with no college degree and limited social experience is at a disadvantage in the corporate structure because of the cultural advantages of the men he will be opposing for top jobs. The man who works his

23

way up inevitably finds it harder adjusting to the corporate life style, often because he resists surrendering preconceived thoughts about "high class" life.

Here is an example. I knew a young man from what sociologists call a lower middle-class background. Yet through his own efforts this man reached the top rung on the middle management level. As he was about to enter the ranks of top management, he was given a Dutch-uncle talk by his superior. He was told how to act and what new social customs to adopt. He was told to join a country club, to take up golf, and to change his style of dress and overall appearance. He was also put forward as a candidate for the exclusive in-town club of the president. The young man came away with a feeling of despair—mainly at the prospect of becoming "high hat" in the eyes of his father and mother for adopting what he had always considered "highfalutin airs." He sensed that if he could not make the transition (and it had to be a fast one) from the old mores of his background to the dictated wishes of his new superiors, he would not get much farther in this particular company.

Of course this is a rather extreme example. The managerial rein on conformity has been loosened in the past few years. Most men in top management realize that there is a new breed of high caliber employees whose differing life-styles pose no threat to the corporation. The point here is that the man who has risen to a new position must be prepared to grapple with the new reality of his position—whether he imagines new superiors pushing him into a new life-style or not.

The Need for More Than Ability

The man who arrives at the top or at the upper middle management level and then realizes that sheer ability is not the only key to success may be in for a rude awakening unless he acquires greater insight into himself and his background. Faced with abandoning a lifelong set of mores, he often finds it difficult to clearly see that a life style must be given up if he is to advance. One must not only adjust but become almost addicted to the habit of terminating old notions and even relationships, because change is a demanding mistress. Because of the stress necessary for any new undertaking, old defense mechanisms must be abandoned and a man must face up to the adoption of a new and suitable behavior pattern.

If, as most psychologists and psychiatrists believe, a man should *not* accept a promotion or move that would "shake him up," require him to make too rapid an adjustment, or cause him to behave in a way that is not comfortable, the business world would lose many men of vision and groundbreaking ability. The security-first emphasis encourages a man to settle for the status quo, and he becomes less and less likely to respond to any urging that would mean a new situation. Of course, many men have a built-in barometer of how much change they feel they can cope with, and are conditioned through prior training to adjust slowly.

Often, however, a man will resist any sudden change. The result is that his final corporate stop in life is lower than he had hoped. Bitter middle management men who have plateaued out are all too common in corporate life.

Stay Flexible in Order to Learn

Psychiatrists and psychologists who coddle men do not fully reflect a hopeful orientation about the capability of man. Of course, many men are paralyzed by years of dedication to an inflexible method of handling life situations, but with the proper support of superiors and friends, it is possible for them to change and to learn a new and more difficult job with many new responsibilities. When a new job opens for a man, he often doubts his ability to do well at the new position. He begins questioning and thinks: "I just don't know whether I can handle this new assignment."

To be sure, some companies and some men promote people without thinking about their prior training or their ability to handle the job. But most companies, when they do promote, assume that the man will grow into the job.

One of the best ways to feel more competent to take on a new job is to review past accomplishments in your business career. Talk to a trusted friend or your wife about what you have achieved in the past and what he or she thinks you can do in the future. Look at your résumé just to remind yourself of the high points and positive achievements in your career. Appraising past performances can both increase your confidence and help you focus on what sort of adjustment you will have to make in the future. The man who becomes more capable also becomes more flexible.

The Positive Use of Anxiety

The seasoned executive knows that as responsibility grows one is pressed harder and that inner, and perhaps hidden, conflicts then emerge and produce stress, which sometimes cannot be either disguised or repressed. If he represses stress, he will not be able to take the next step—adding more responsibilities. But if he chooses to deal with the resultant anxiety, he can move to the next plateau. At the very least, he will be capable of more growth. It is no accident that one often hears a person, reflecting his own anxiety about increased responsibility, say: How in the world can he do it? For example, how could the late President John F. Kennedy handle the responsibility of a family and the most trying job in the world and still find time to play hard, work at hobbies, and maintain other interests?

Unfortunately, anxiety is for the most part viewed as a sign of weakness both in management circles and society in general. Because of our social mores, anxiety is downgraded and we tend to stress textbook talk of self-reliance and courage. Our desire to conform to the prevailing prestige standards or current social dicta causes us to hide the existence of this tension so necessary for continued movement. Therefore the emphasis on being "cool," so that an objective decision, or at least a detached one, can be reached. Being cool does not necessarily mean that a better decision can be made, because often one omits possible vital factors by dissociating or avoiding the anxiety that these factors produce. What I am saying is that tension or anxiety in a job is not socially allowable, even though a high percentage of unseen "gut" emotions go into most executive decisions.

I am not saying that when a man takes the stage to speak he should lose control of all the "cool" necessary to deliver the speech. I do feel that one must first recognize the importance and function of anxiety and learn to use it to best advantage.

Perhaps the best examples of stress are the physical symptoms before any sort of combat, be it physical or mental. Many an experienced executive speaker feels his palms sweat before a major speech, just as a soldier before battle has a dry mouth and a tense stomach. These are involuntary versions of what an athlete does in "psyching" himself up before a contest. All the possibilities of action soon to come flash through the mind, accompanied by an increased flow of adrenaline. Studies have shown that the soldier who is aware of the inevitability of this particular state of mind, and who does not dissociate the feeling involved, is more apt to survive in battle.

Those who avoid situations that elicit vague feelings of dread are so rooted in their own despair at the possibility of coping that they retreat. That is probably why many top executives, or men with larger responsibilities, yearn for "the simple life." These men wish they did not have to face the consequences or responsibility for their own forward movement in life: that is, job, family, friendship. Not all people experience anxiety or tension, but those who do and deal with it move ahead in any given field or situation because they are willing to venture beyond what is already known or previously experienced. They are the groundbreakers and leaders. They do not accept a personal status quo.

Changing Conditions in Corporations

What about the person who is free of anxiety or who does not have apprehensions about acting upon new conditions? True, some are better equipped by early childhood and subsequent experience to comfortably move into new life circumstances. However, I believe that this is not true of the overwhelming majority of a population born into what W. H. Auden has called "the age of anxiety."

But let us turn specifically to the individual in a

corporate setting. The dichotomy between the business ethic and the social ethic has become blurred because of growing pressures on business from outside social forces. In addition to the confusion over a mixed business and social ethic, there is another unsettling new phenomenon—the speed with which the top executive arrives in the presidential suite. The average age of a company president is now under 50—49, to be precise—where just 10 years ago it was 56. So we have the phenomenon of men in a hurry arriving faster, carrying the baggage of accumulated tensions acquired very fast. In the past, such tensions were largely eliminated during the developmental stage in a man's career. Now, however, there are fewer outlets (despite the increase in "leisure time") and less free time to help a man figure out where he is headed and what he really wants in life. I would imagine that this will lead to more young people achieving great monetary success in our society, but that there will be an undercurrent of dissatisfaction and a feeling that some real needs have been ignored on the way to the corporate heights.

Social Concerns Versus Corporate Reality

Let me try to explain what I mean by increased social pressures coming to bear on business ethics to produce what might be termed a confrontation with the minds of bright young men. With companies under pressure to deal with such current concerns as ecology, pollution, and consumer safety, the reasons for corporate existence become somewhat obscured. More and more major companies are assigning officers to handle social problems. Companies that perhaps began with minority job programs progress to concern over pollution. Some have made an attempt to recognize the equality of women in deed as well as in word. And it's to be hoped that corporations will continue the trend to social concern.

But what corporations state and what they practice may be two different policies, and a corporate backlash against consumerism may be on the way. A General Motors Corporation statement of 1970 vintage notes: "A corporation can only discharge its obligation to society if it continues to be a profitable investment for its stockholders." (General Motors has already changed its policy of defensiveness about its products.)

The forward-looking young man must never forget that a company's first and unyielding goal is profit. It serves the *majority* of its shareholders—despite what copywriters say in annual reports and what window dressing vice-presidents put forth at urban or social-problem seminars.

Correspondence between two corporate power wielders provides a rare glimpse at the strict business ethic in practice. This is Alfred P. Sloan (then president of General Motors) writing to Lammot du Pont (then president of E. I. du Pont de Nemours & Company) on the question of whether or not to equip GM cars with the new safety glass developed by Du Pont: "I would very much rather spend the same amount of money in improving our car in other ways because I think, from the standpoint of selfish business, it would be a much better investment. You can say, perhaps, that I am selfish, but *business is selfish. We are not a charitable institution—we are trying to make a profit for our stockholders.*" * (Italics mine.) The cor-

* Quoted in Morton Mintz and Jerry S. Cohen, *America, Inc.: Who Owns and Operates the United States* (New York: Dial Press, 1971).

respondence took place over 30 years ago, but similar
sentiment remains strong in corporate boardrooms.

I believe that a great percentage of the stress af-
fecting the middle management executive is rooted in
deprivation or a lack of recognition of real needs,
some societal, some self-imposed. So if you blame the
boss (or your company) for your problems and tensions and he is removed, chances are that you will
find fault with the next boss or company if you have
not rooted out the real cause of your disgruntlement.
This, as many social scientists have pointed out, is
usually a failure to clearly understand your business
goals and the motivations behind them.

The Big Decision

Our educational institutions teach very lofty ideas,
including the golden rule, but later, as almost everyone
acknowledges, there is a rude awakening to the facts of
life—especially in the business arena.

Nothing jars a young manager more than a personal
make-or-break decision. Whatever the decision, the
choice is almost always evaluated by superiors. How
you react to the final hurdle, which may be placed in
your way deliberately, will determine your course in
the business world, and particularly in your current
company.

Often the "testing" for top executive ability can
be quite subtle. I know of a "bright young man" who
zoomed through the ranks to a position just below the
upper echelon. He was performing well at his newest
job and was anxiously awaiting recognition from a
power-wielding vice-president, the man who could
make or break his career. Suddenly, the test came.
He was invited to lunch with the vice-president, with

no particular topic on the agenda—ostensibly they would have a general discussion of his department. While the young man was busy trying to figure out ways to put his best foot forward, his superior had much more important matters to discuss. On the way to his posh private club, the vice-president casually asked the younger man why he was still living in the city. The young man replied: "Oh, I don't know, I still enjoy it. Most of my friends live here and my wife's work is here." He did not realize the older executive was testing him to see if he would readily abandon his present life-style and adopt one that the corporation felt was appropriate for its top executive echelon. The senior executive then chatted about the advantages of suburban living. Fortunately for most companies, the ambitious executive can hardly wait to move into the suburbs. This young man proved to be no exception.

This preliminary feeling out of a man's ambitiousness to determine if he is open or committed to a top executive value system is very important. But what if the young man answered his questioner quite openly and frankly? What if he told the senior executive that he did not want to get caught up in a keeping-up-with-the-Joneses prestige system which would afford him no choices as he became further and further enmeshed in it? What if the young man felt nervous about buying and maintaining a home in the suburbs even while his salary was increased? Perhaps he feared the security trap. What if he did not want to be in the position that so many executives found themselves in during the recession of 1969 through 1971—so dependent on the company that they were afraid to make a move outside or were paralyzed when they lost their jobs? Corporations do encourage dependency on their beneficence and can act as the sole satisfier of a person's needs.

Let's look at another example of key decision making. A junior and senior man are at lunch. They engage in innocuous conversation. Then they get down to the nitty-gritty. The senior man adjusts his chair and directly confronts the junior. His conversation begins: "We've been doing a lot of thinking, Jack, about the problem of the XYZ product and your department. We've decided that you're going to do this for us." Now the junior man recognizes that if he does not comply with this order, he may dampen his chances for any further promotion. If he accepts what he perceives to be a distasteful proposition, he will perhaps move to the next step on the ladder. If he does not, he may be doomed to his present position on the table of organization, with nothing more than a chance at a lateral move. (The man frozen in position may be reprieved by a change in top management, but most new men bring their own cadre with them.) At the same time, he thinks about his prospects at any other company—and realizes the same thing would probably happen there. He has suddenly confronted the impersonal character of the business world. If he is to advance, he must decide to "play the game."

Usually a situation will not be as naked as the example used here. There is usually a middle way that can be found between the position of the senior man and that of the eager junior, but the latter must convince his superior of that. Most first-rate executives realize that reasoned dissent within the decision-making councils is allowable and even necessary.

But the extreme illustration above points up how important a single major decision can be to a career. It also illustrates a major stress problem that will almost inevitably arise in a young executive's push to arrive at the boardroom.

Coming to Grips with Your Feelings

We have discussed stress as being inherent in a system that for the most part holds that the ends justify the means. Most men, after recovering from the initial jolt of recognizing this fact, move to deal with the gap between the narrow demands of the company and their personal needs. That is why most management consultants ask what a man's outside interests are. They stress that for personal satisfaction it is important to maintain contacts outside business. Obviously, a person's attitude or prevailing mood can vitally affect his performance within a company.

To break out of a mood of indifference or avoidance, consult with a person who is not directly involved with your predilection for footdragging. Perhaps an older man who has adjusted to his own plateau in the company can be of service.

By plugging into some sort of feedback outlet, you can best determine corporate "reality." If you reconcile that reality with your own life pattern, you can better anticipate and react.

This chapter has tried to focus on the feelings that surface as one attempts to scale the corporate heights. It is well to remember that you are solely responsible for your life. Think and plan it well. As George Bernard Shaw said: "You don't hold your own in the world by standing on guard, but by attacking, and getting well hammered yourself."

THE NECESSITY FOR PEER GROUP COMPATIBILITY 3

The vast majority of management books totally ignore the importance of peer group relationships in the corporate organizational structure—which is astounding considering that most of the time spent by anyone in a company is spent with that person's peers.

Perhaps management experts have pooh-poohed the subject of peer group activity and concentrated on unequal relationships such as superior to subordinate, or subordinate to superior, because they have not considered the question of equal relationships in a business hierarchy relevant. Most studies reflect a failure to appreciate the fact that what a man learns in one peer group will be valuable to him in new peer groups. For one thing, peer compatibility demands more tact and sensitivity than the other relationships (superior to subordinate, subordinate to superior) because a man's performance in his immediate group largely determines his relationship to the organization as a whole. It is the same in society at large. The child who has trouble dealing with peers, who are necessary for his support and growth, will later find it difficult to consider himself a free individual in the larger society. He will always feel dependent on some sort of authority figure or institution to tell him how to live. In other words, he will play the role of dependent child.

Another reason why management pundits usually avoid the topic of peer relationships is because they tend to discount the forms of competitiveness that develop within the group. How a man copes with such competition often determines how he will fare in any other group that he then advances to, including the top executive stratum. What follows in this chapter is devoted to lifting you gracefully out of your current peer group and transporting you to another as painlessly as possible.

Some Facts About Peer Groups

It is no accident that in Western society, man is judged by his peers, the best example being the jury system. The Magna Carta, as good a statement as any of how peer groups must function, includes the following: "No freeman shall be taken, or imprisoned, or outlawed, or exiled, or in any way harmed, nor will we go upon him nor will we send upon him, except by the legal judgment by his peers or by the law of the land." Peer group power is well established in practice and precedent.

One of the major problems in discussing peer groups, as they function in the corporate world, is that a distinction must be made, however tentatively, about peer groups in our society. All too often a peer is defined by measures other than personal living competence. In other words, company presidents associate with

36

other company presidents because of an emphasis on prestige factors rather than because of personal compatibility. The millionaire in our society is rarely a close friend of the gardener on his estate. The Princeton man who tries to join a blue-collar bowling league to be "one of the boys" soon encounters problems. To be a peer, one must experience others as being like himself. If, because of the layers of social garments he has clothed himself with, he does not, it will be almost impossible for him to join a group—any group.

Competition Among Peers

One of the major reasons why the nature of competition in peer groups is played down is obvious: New groups do not take kindly to you if you have established yourself as "cutthroat" on a lower level. In other words, top echelon executives, if they see a too obviously competitive man on a middle level, assume he will continue in character when he reaches their level. It is not likely that such a man would adopt the more subtle forms of competitiveness needed as one rises in an organization. One must clearly understand that the majority of time in a corporate organization, and in most instances in the larger society as well, is spent in contact with people on one's own level. In an organization one talks not to superiors, but to those considered one's equals. Of course, they may be equal only on an organizational chart, for there are always informal leaders in peer groups.

Working well with a peer group on a middle management level is essential, but one must be ready to adjust to a more dynamic style when one is promoted to a higher echelon. If you are an impatient man who shows many of the characteristics of top leadership, you will become aware of the problem of personality shifting. Say you are presently on a middle management level: you must exhibit such characteristics as caution, calmness, modesty, and patience. But when you eventually move to top management, you will have to be creative, driving, decisive, and ready to assume greater responsibility—and many a middle management man has floundered on entering the ranks of top management because he has not prepared himself for the transition.

Some top management men have bandied about the idea of a training course for middle managers who are about to enter top management levels. And there already are programs in various corporations that serve the same functional purpose. If, as numerous studies show, middle managers are more defensive and submissive than the men who rule them from above, how are they to survive the developmental stage of middle management with enough of their individuality intact to proceed upward? The functions learned in peer group experience that serve to define and differentiate the individual on the middle management level are invaluable to the man who is able to master them.

The Paradox of Nonconformity

The big problem for a middle management man is how to be a maverick and yet not destroy his career before it is launched. He must somehow show the boss that he is a creative thinker and doer, and, while standing out from his peers, must win their support without incurring their enmity. And where is he to come from when most corporations search for the "well-adjusted" trainee (a euphemism for the nonchallenger) or what they often label a "nontroublemaker"? The irony here is that no company president is ever called a trouble-maker; he is always an innovator. But until a man becomes a corporate leader it is difficult for him to be an experimenter and survive. The trouble is that while the placid or well-adjusted individual may be an industrious worker, he is not necessarily a leader. Quite often the well-adjusted are not drivers. They just want to fit in, not rock the boat, and for the most part are what psychologists would term dependent personalities.

Now that we have discussed the extremely important role of peers, let us try to pick out specific areas that should be explored in peer group situations.

Constructive Versus Destructive Competition

One of the key areas is competition. Again, if you understand the nature of competition among your constant companions, you will be able to bolster your ability to compete on another, higher, level. But competition can be destructive as well as constructive. For example, it is important to recognize an office situation where competition has become counterproductive or is simply being overstressed. You can perceive this by noting whether unrealistic goals (sales quotas, production performance, memo deadlines, and so forth) are the rule rather than the exception. Extreme competitiveness will also be apparent in excessive visual reminders, such as charts and graphs, and in too high an incidence of meetings, harangues, and pep talks. Covert alliances, while less noticeable, are also a strong indication of an unhealthy competitive atmosphere. In addition to fostering needless competition among peers, such situations keep young executives from learning the importance of compromise and cooperation, so necessary for leadership on a higher level. In other words, this sort of office atmosphere encourages bickering and backstabbing among men who should be preparing themselves for the elite management circle.

Another management tactic that can lead to destructive competition in the middle management ranks, and common during economic recessions, is a memo from the front office stipulating across-the-board job cuts of x percent in each division—this, with no prior consultation with any lower level managers. Such tactics reflect either laziness or a failure to recognize that each division and, if possible, each person should be treated on an individual basis.

In at least one kind of atmosphere where constructive competition thrives, the manager discusses obtainable goals—goals that have been set by the group, not handed down from on high. The only controls are those set by the group, and each individual is encouraged to work at his own pace. Of course this sort of open corporate situation will remain extremely rare until top management abandons its generally pessimistic view that the worker must be pushed or prodded into producing. No salesman should have to follow an office schedule that, for example, makes client calls mandatory between 9:30 and 10:00. What if a client is never in at those hours? What if the client does not speak to salesmen in the morning? If one is to cater to a client's needs, there should be no formal structure. Each man should be free to set his own schedule, secure in the knowledge that what counts is the final line on the profit and loss statement.

But even given a cooperative situation, the question remains: How do you set yourself apart while not antagonizing your group? Before we answer that, let's consider the elements that are involved. First of all, if one learns only as he is forced out of safe, routine behavior so that he acquires new patterns in new situations, then the middle management peer group can be seen as a sort of testing place or developmental stage. Entry into a new group is crucial, because first impressions do linger. Therefore don't make strong demands or express contradictory opinions about present group functions and activities when you first appear on the scene. If you do, you are in effect saying to a group that has been functioning for some time: ''Look fellows, this is all wrong. Why don't we do it this way?''

Another facet of peer compatibility is the emphasis on cooperating rather than on competing. A defiant stance, which only suggests that you think everyone is out to get you, must be dropped. The ''lone wolf'' attitude, reinforced by a growing paranoia, very rarely leads a man to the top. A man may keep his own counsel, but he still needs the open support of his fellows if he is to take the next step.

How to Do Well in a Peer Group

Here are a number of ways that one can win acceptance from one's peers while still doing the sort of job that will be noticed by superiors. First of all, be cooperative. Studies show that if a group pursues a common goal, one of the byproducts will be a reduction of competitive prejudice within the group. This is particularly true if the goal shared by the group is officially sanctioned by the company. Learning exactly how another person pursues a goal is one way to replace animosity with instruction.

Here is an example of institutionalized goal setting for management. On becoming president of Pullman

Inc. in 1970, Samuel B. Casey, Jr. promptly circulated a memo stating that he had already submitted his own resignation to the company effective December 1, 1980. He thus put the young men on notice that his job would be available. Of course much can happen between now and 1980, but the memo is a good example of how Casey united management by rallying them around a common cause—pursuit of his job.

When you realize that cooperation in a company is a method for establishing real skills, you will also realize that you are cooperating in order to compete within a system of selection and promotion. The middle manager competes for preference within the corporate framework of cooperation—that is, his unit or his division. The company itself may be similarly competing —for it may be part of a conglomerate. So be forewarned that personal ambitions must be reined until you are in a position high enough to be more obvious.

Let's assume that you have established a comfortable relationship with your middle management group, for if you have, you can then display some maverick qualities. Of course, such qualities, though necessary for top management leadership, may be considered "way out" on a middle management level. If your attempt to stand out from your immediate group fails to elicit encouragement and support, you must be prepared to withstand the slings and arrows of outrageous peers. But you will eventually have to make waves to be noticed for your leadership qualities and gain the new experience necessary to prepare you for more responsibility.

Don't Run to the Boss

One way to blunt peer antagonism is to shy away from the appeal to authority. Never settle a dispute by rushing prematurely to a superior when you can settle your differences within the group. If you go outside the group too often, you will acquire a reputation as a crybaby.

There are many such situations in the business world —as, for instance, the secretary who cries to her boss about being left out of secretarial lunches. A sympathetic boss may at first listen, and even try to make some conciliatory move, but eventually he will start to wonder why she cannot work out interpersonal problems with her friends. The same thing happens in a middle management peer group.

If such a group sees that one of their number is constantly going to the boss, they will begin to ostracize him. Not only will the offender lose the respect of his immediate companions, but his boss will begin to view him as a man not capable of functioning at his proper level.

One of the byproducts of a man's being a corporation maverick is that he is usually acknowledged as being ambitious, driving, and able. Yet his dissatisfaction at being on a lower level sometimes leads to difficulty in adjusting to people in his group who have "settled down." In fact, the maverick generally tends to create problems. This leads to the corporate predicament of acknowledging that he has talent while at the same time stifling him. As a result, a corporation often deprives itself of the productive dissatisfied member because it fails to properly utilize him—usually because it fears the reaction of the maverick's peer group. In other words, most corporations are afraid that people on a lower level will become disgruntled if the company recognizes a person who has achieved a sort of maverick status among them. What usually happens is that the corporation drops the maverick in the interests of not threatening the status quo. Neither are the top members of the corporate hierarchy eager to welcome a maverick on their own level. They sense that he will not adjust to their style and sensibilities once he gains entrance. Yet many a corporation has regretted firing a talented middle manager who has joined another company that not only accepts his life style but capitalizes on it. So once more we see a paradox inherent in the corporate structure—a paradox a man must recognize if he is to move ahead.

Concentrate on Cooperation

Let us return to our discussion of how best to relate to peers as basic training for rapid advancement. Another illustration might serve us well here. When I was editor-in-chief of a business magazine, there were many problems about coordinating editorial direction with advertising goals. To solve such problems I communicated directly with the advertising manager. I found it quite helpful. When I could tell him in advance about particular stories that we were planning to run that might touch sensitive areas, we were able to figure out a plan should a certain advertiser be upset. The cooperative effort was much more rewarding than the usual editorial-advertising battle, and yet it neither endangered editorial excellence nor deprived the industry of the news it needed and had a right to see. By working closely together we avoided going directly to the publisher and thereby putting him on the spot.

One of the keys to functioning well with peers is the empathic ability to sort out what a person wants and then to offer him a way to achieve it while at the same time furthering your own particular cause. To do that requires a desire to know whom you are working with and what their interests are. For example, if you know that a man's hobby is writing, and he is a member of one of your committees, you have prior information that would more than likely help you persuade him to accept the job of preparing the committee's written reports. If you're aware of the personal interests and ambitions of co-workers it can help you determine how best to approach them. When asking a favor or aid on a particular project that may be important to you, always approach them with their best interests, not yours, in mind. In that way, a spirit of cooperation prevails and the focus is on a common goal. Instead of developing a resentful "I'm working for him" attitude, they can feel a sense of participation.

One thing never to do in peer group situations is to embarrass another man or point out his mistakes, be it at a meeting, at a conference, or in a situation where three or four people are sitting around in an office. The man may not comment at the time, but he will remember it. Later, he may choose to withdraw support for a pet project of yours or subtly sabotage it.

Strive for personal diplomacy in conferences, because that is a major yardstick by which peers measure a man's competence. If the group has to choose a spokesman and it knows that you are capable in a conference, it will turn to you. In that way you will have won group sanction for an activity that can boost your standing with superiors.

Don't acquire the "goldbrick" label. Any man who delegates details to peers that he should handle himself can only hurt his reputation and breed resentment. And be careful not to postpone attending to details by assuming that they are someone else's responsibility.

One of the major considerations in a group is that of

alliances. When you do make close friendships, be careful not to shut out other members. Remain open for consultation and friendship because if they think you've entered an exclusive alliance they will tend to shun you.

Be True to Your Group

Another very important aspect of building up group faith in you is to make it clear that you are not ordinarily on management's side, that you are with the group and subscribe to the code it has informally adopted. One of the toughest management problems for a middle manager is to keep subordinates from believing that he is interested only in the company. He must constantly keep subordinates aware, genuinely so, that he is interested in their welfare just as much as that of the company. The same principle holds in a peer group: You must combine a genuine feeling for and loyalty to the group with a greater loyalty to yourself—a loyalty that may coincide with the interests of the company. If you have established a firm position in the group and retain this loyalty to yourself, then, should you be forced to choose between the company and the group, you will be able to choose the company with a clear conscience. Nor will you leave the group feeling guilty about having "used" the other members.

Another characteristic that most groups applaud in a member is honesty joined to consistency; if a group always knows what your position is on an issue, be it company policy, or politics, or anything else, then they can admire you even if they don't agree with what you believe. If, however, you have a reputation as a man who is constantly changing his mind, you will be roundly damned. A gentle way to make your convictions known to someone else is to first listen and then gently ask questions about his own stand on the same subject. Never appear angry and reject his views outright by saying "No, I think that's absolutely wrong." You can lead him to a better understanding and a sense of what you are thinking through non-threatening conversation. Even if you do not convince him at that time, he will remember what you said. If, on the other hand, he reacts angrily to your tone, the chances are that he will not hear the reason in your arguments. Yet once you manage to implant your ideas tactfully, he may indeed change his thinking. (If he is a man who needs to save face, he will shift positions at a later date.) The successful diplomat always allows the other man as many options as possible, so that he can withdraw or change his position, even if ever so slightly, without feeling embarrassed.

Observe the Group's Informal Rules

Now let us assume that you are firmly rooted in a group and are ready to be noticed by superiors. One of the ways to reach outside the group and demonstrate what top management regards as a sure sign of leadership is to volunteer. Management's volunteer syndrome says that anyone who volunteers for extra work must be capable of leadership. It may not necessarily follow, but in any case it is a quality much admired by top management. The only problem with volunteering is that it's a competitive strategy. One bumps up against the informal rule structure set by the peer group. If your group frowns upon extra work, you will be castigated for working overtime (when you should be out with the boys, or home with your children, or whatever).

The clearest example of group pressure to conform is the hours of factory workers. Even if a man on the line is engrossed in some facet of his job, he immediately stops working when he hears the buzzer signaling a break. He may be in the middle of a project, but even if he wanted to finish it—and I believe most men would like to finish—he is afraid of pressure from his group. If he shows up in the canteen area two minutes after the others to find them already sitting having coffee, and he can only say apologetically that he wanted to finish a particular soldering job, most likely he will be made to feel guilty. He could also be the object of some derision.

One's freedom to change is enhanced by adapting to a particular group and then introducing changes that do not threaten the group with disintegration. When you leave a group to assume a higher position in a company, it must be made clear that you will remain "available." In that way, you will maintain group support and avoid the hostility that would result if the group members felt you had abandoned them.

How to Change Patterns in a Group

As in the group, it is most important that one fit into the activities of an organization before he can be effective in changing the informal pattern of rules. This has been documented in a study entitled "Group Leadership and Institutionalization." * In this study of children's play groups, Ferenc Merei noted patterns of activity with children. After it was observed who was the leader of each group, that child was removed

---

* Ferenc Merei, "Group Leadership and Institutionalization," in E. Maccoby, T. Newcomb, and E. Hartley, eds., *Readings in Social Psychology* (New York: Henry Holt and Company, 1958).

from the group. A new leader then took over and the group established a slightly different pattern of behavior. When Merei brought back the former leader, the latter had to modify his behavior to the new pattern and was not able to initiate new activities. In fact, when he attempted to act as in the past, he was either resisted or ignored. He first had to reestablish himself by conforming to the new group pattern. Only after the children responded to him on that level was he able to introduce activities that had not been tried previously. This illustrates quite vividly the importance of fitting in with group patterns before attempting to lead.

It seems self-evident that isolationists do not emerge as top managers: A leader must have a group to interact with. At the same time, he must share common goals with his followers so that they will accept their subordinate role. The two roles are interdependent, and interdependency flows from a mutual acceptance.

Since mutual acceptance is learned in the give-and-take of peer group interaction, the man who first uttered "I would not ask my men to do anything that I did not do" understood a major principle of how to attain leadership. He certainly understood the compelling need for peer group compatibility.

HOW TO MAINTAIN
A HIGH PROFILE

4

An anonymous corporate observer once cynically remarked that the intensely ambitious man either becomes a company president or is fired early in his career. As stark as this assessment may appear, it often describes the sad reality for the bright and ambitious man who has not learned to effectively promote himself.

Just how does one maintain a "high profile"? First, let us differentiate between a negative and a positive high profile. Obviously a negative one can destroy a career before it is properly launched. Remember that we compete in a system that likes its competitiveness covered with a veneer of affability, which more often than not has the durability of gossamer.

Your profile begins to be established from your first interview on—when your dossier becomes an open book for executives. This chapter will try to guide you in making sure that positive material lands in that dossier—material that can help lead to rapid promotions. To be sure, top executives, when considering a man for promotion, rarely look at his personnel file. There is, however, a tendency to trot out a person's dossier when looking for a reason for *not* offering a promotion. So be forewarned: It pays to have positive references in your file—even if only as a deterrent to a wily top executive looking to deny you a new position. Certain gentlemen have been known to select one or two small but negative items in a man's background as justification for denying him a deserved raise or move.

Remember, high visibility does not always mean a positive image. It can just as easily produce a negative one.

A prime example of profile- or image-making can be seen in the style of President Richard M. Nixon. His tactics reflect the double-edged risks of high profile-manship. As President he can commandeer prime television time on short notice, or request and receive an audience with powerful media representatives. It is no accident that many of his early key advisers came from the advertising ranks and were professionals in the use of time and exposure to ''sell'' any chosen image. One's personal feelings aside, Mr. Nixon's use of the momentous moon landing as a vehicle to reach millions of viewers (through his telephone call to the astronauts) was a most obvious instance of high profilism. Going ''direct to the people'' may infuriate other elected representatives, as was the case in the handling of the 1970 Cambodian ''incursion,'' but the President was able to instantly communicate his version of events to a mass audience. Such visibility could be compared, at a more prosaic level, to having your picture taken with the company president at the annual company picnic. When the president looks at the pictures in his office a couple of weeks later, he notices the man near him in the photo, turns to his executive assistant and says, "Just who is that man and what does he do?" That is planting an image in the mind of a man who can help you.

It is also worth noting that although the importance of high visibility in a corporation is not changing, the elements and tactics are. For example, the wife's role in the visibility strategy is rapidly being transformed because of the movement by women to alter not only their relation to our society but also our institutions' methods of relating to them. We no longer will see the quiet, attuned wife, content merely to purr quietly at her husband's side. An active corporate wife is emerging, one who can be a thorn in an ambitious man's side, but who makes herself heard. As the decade progresses she will become increasingly important. And she will take an even more active role in the community. Indeed, she has already begun to challenge —outside the confines of her usual domestic scene— some of the basic premises of our business and technological mores.

The maintenance of a high profile in a company requires a two-pronged attack: one aimed at reaching superiors who are in a position to advance your career, the other at attuning yourself to the company.

Methods of adapting to a boss are discussed in detail in Chapter 5, "Sizing Up Superiors," but let's highlight some major points.

One, try to complement your boss's personality— but also emphasize your strong points. Steer conversation to topics of interest to him that you also have an interest in. Most bosses feel more comfortable talking to subordinates about topics not directly related to the company, such as rising prices, maintaining houses in the suburbs, and schooling.

Begin to zero in on your company's policies and objectives so that your own actions will be in accord with them. Begin to make decisions on each level you're concerned with. Even if you haven't been briefed on the company's long-range or overall objectives, you certainly should have an inkling of what they are.

Find Company Objectives and Work from Them

If you are unclear on your company's objectives, there are ways to find out what they are. When you do not have access to the company president or are not important enough to attend top level meetings, information can be gleaned from annual reports and from speeches delivered by top men at various meetings. For example, you can obtain transcripts of security analyst meetings, where the company optimistically presents its plans and its philosophy to the men who sell to and tell the stock-buying public about the company.

Other sources include newspaper reports, and new policy directives, which should be taken seriously, not just stuffed into the nearest wastebasket. Stories in your industry's trade journals are also a good source for discovering changes in a company's attitudes and objectives. Very often an astute journalist will find out about a company's intended moves well before they are announced publicly.

Still other information sources include company-sponsored brochures, which carry the company "line" to the public, in-house organs, and supplementary or quarterly reports. Full texts of speeches made by major figures in the corporation can usually be found in the public relations office. Perhaps a company librarian can help.

Once you have determined what the company's goals are, you can begin to adjust your everyday behavior. Start by making yourself valuable to your company from the outside in. Become involved in trade association work. As dull as association labor may seem, the opportunity for exposure within an industry can lead to recognition within your own company. Be quick to establish that you are available for quotation on industry problems in trade journals and are also interested in publishing yourself (if you can get permission to do so). If you are active in your industry, it may happen that a competitor will mention your name to one of your superiors. You may not be doing a great job on the inside, but if you are much sought after on the outside, your boss will be reluctant to let you go when you are offered another job—if only for prestige reasons.

In fact, there are many companies that have some very well-paid senior men who do nothing but relate outside the company. These companies rarely fire these men, for they have become "institutions." It would hurt the company image and the men would probably immediately sign on with an arch rival. These men have succeeded in making themselves needed for any number of reasons; and although they may never become president, they are usually close to the top. Of course, some "industry figures" or "trade association men" are often just waiting for retirement.

With company objectives firmly in mind, select pertinent meetings or conferences and manage to attend them. See if you can get appointed to various committees that exist in more than name and that issue reports that are widely read. If possible, as a committee member, make some of your feelings or ideas known in a report that bears your name or at least mentions you. Be willing to accept a menial job—one that may make up for its triviality with a high visibility factor.

There are many stories of office boys who have risen rapidly in a company because they had access to top men who became their supporters. Top echelon men could hardly feel threatened by an office boy, and I believe that is one of the key reasons such individuals move into the company system rapidly once they find a sponsor. Your position on the middle level, however, is not quite the same thing. The point is that if you make yourself available at any number of functions where there is likely to be a cross section of people you would not ordinarily contact, it can aid your cause.

Learn from the office boy's method for working his way into the system: he is so far down the ladder that he feels no compulsion to appear to know everything. Therefore, he is not afraid to ask questions of superiors. This is a habit that is frequently lost as one scales the corporate heights. Most men feel that as they progress in a corporation, they should not ask questions—this, for fear either of being labeled dumb or of appearing not to know their job. This is an outgrowth of a desire to see authority as all-knowing. This myth should be exorcised by any man who expects to continue to grow and mature on a job and prepare himself for his next assignment. Do not stop asking questions, particularly when you need advice. Become advice-prone. Nothing is more flattering—in the best sense of the word. When you seek advice you are able to ask a sincere question and a boss is able to give you a straight and helpful answer. It leads to satisfaction for both parties. In addition, if you go out and enthusiastically do what the man advised, you are certainly going to proceed with his implicit obligation to help you fulfill the suggested course of action. I know of many men who give advice to subordinates and then go out of their way to help them carry it out. Since asking advice is a form of flattery, however, do not overdo it. Do not bother your boss with inconsequential questions. Shrewd executives are quick to separate sincere opinion seekers from obvious apple polishers.

In fact, correctly perceiving how much or when to approach a superior in your quest for high visibility can be crucial. Let's say you are at an important meeting and the division head presents a new company directive or makes a short speech outlining fresh goals. He then talks about the philosophy involved. Not many questions are asked at the meeting; it's basically a presentation. Or perhaps you are attending an industry function where a senior member of the company has just made a speech to the members of the group. In either case, should you approach the speaker to comment?

If you feel that the speech was rather perfunctory and the man who gave it was not "fired up," don't dash up to him and gush about his effectiveness. You can judge how his speech was received by audience reaction. If he seems relieved that it's over, stay away from him. Let the other juniors approach him with whatever they want to say. If he perceives that you are approaching him just to flatter him, he will quickly mark you as an opportunist. Perhaps a better or more suitable reaction on your part might be to wait a day or two. If possible, find a copy of the speech or presentation or refer to any notes you may have taken. Concentrate your pre-meeting thoughts on an area in which you have some expertise and then find a way to approach the man. Perhaps an opening could be: "I was just thinking about your speech (or presentation) and was particularly struck by the following . . ." At that point you can either agree and then perhaps make a suggestion for adding something to the presentation, or you can, in a minor way, take exception to what was said. If you do take exception, be sure to offer an alternative.

You might feel more comfortable sending a note commenting on the speech or presentation. This allows the speechmaker time to digest initial reaction and it also makes him aware that you have been thinking about what he said. You fix in his mind the notion that you took time to think about and to comment on what he had said or presented.

The Nuances of Competition

Don't confuse clear visibility with irritating density. Restrain the tendency to react with false enthusiasm to a superior's speech. The problem of proper and well-timed restraint crops up in a corporation because of unclear attitudes toward competitiveness within the system. You compete with fellow members of a structure while seemingly not competing with them directly. Ostensibly you compete for a higher position, but you cannot forget that you are competing directly on an equal level for the upper position.

One can talk about outdoing another person outside his group, but it is *verboten* to openly outdo someone in one's immediate circle. If you are not clear on this built-in corporate ambiguity, you will suffer unnecessary conflicts about goals and methods of achieving them.

For example, on a bowling team outside the immediate corporate environment, one is lauded for helping beat the other team, because they are "the other guys." But competition applied to your own team is decried because one does not *openly* compete with members of the same team.

Often a competitive person is confused as to when open competition is acceptable and when it is not. In the corporate scene the problem is particularly touchy because it is difficult to conceal the fact that you are trying to outdo or replace the people with whom you are working.

Frequently, superiors foster stressful competition and then accuse you of being competitive. Of course, they are right, so be clear that the nature of the quest requires you to be aggressive and competitive. Often, when a superior or competitor accuses you of being pushy, it is because he feels threatened. He is playing on your inner fear of appearing to be an open competitor in a system that is held up as being noncompetitive. Indeed, while some firms appear easygoing, every company that I have ever been associated with or have heard about is competitive—it has to be because of the nature of the free enterprise system in which we function.

Suppose one day you are "broken" for being overly competitive. Perhaps you deserve the dressing down that you have gotten. But do not let this experience induce you to give up. If need be, get out of the company. Often a top executive befriends you when he hints that your attitude will not lead to greater glory in his company. Learn from this experience and move to another company where aggressiveness is rewarded. If it isn't, perhaps by then you will have learned how to be more subtle in your interactions with people within the structure of the company's personality.

Should You Build Your Own Empire?

One of the other routes open to the maintenance of a high profile (and also to controversy) is empire building. Some managers feel secure with a large cadre of loyalists surrounding them in a department; others feel hindered.

I believe that one should avoid the practice. Do not build your own Balkan empire, because it will eventually become too unwieldly. In addition, if it is tabbed as counterproductive by superiors, it could become a millstone when you want to disassociate yourself from it to accept another position or move up in the company. If you have built a department that is largely dependent or your presence, superiors will be reluctant to replace you with someone who does not know the situation as well as you do.

The most reliable method for advancement remains that of being your own man—able to shift with changes, not dependent on a substructure created by yourself, and not in a position of having to feel guilty because you have others depending on you when you leave.

Self-reliance sidesteps empire-inspired alliances and symbiotic dependencies. If you attach yourself closely to one man, he may proceed up the ladder and take you along with him. If he falls, however, you'll probably fall with him. So be careful of riding someone else's coattails. If he slips, you had better be able to move away and avoid being pulled down with him.

With the emphasis on executive search companies slated to become even more of a factor in the 1970s job market, previously invisible middle managers must strive to become noticeable. Because of increased competition, many an executive recruiter complains that too few middle echelon men are seen or heard. The recruiter must "see" you so he can contact you for upward placement with a client.

Tips on Future Contacts

Here are a few more techniques that might lead to an unannounced and ego-building call from an executive recruiter. Do not sever old relationships unnecessarily. If possible, remain on good terms with old bosses. Maintaining friendship with equal-level people can be of help. Who can tell when an old friend at another company will be asked if he knows anybody who can handle a particular job? He could just as easily recommend you as anyone else.

Be open with friends you trust. If a friend is approached by another company or a "headhunter," he may not be looking for a job, but would certainly be aware of your plight. In all probability, he will tell the recruiter that he is not interested, but will mention that he knows someone who is.

Even alumni magazines can be helpful. If possible, maintain contact with various school publications. Not only will your classmates see your name, but they may want to contact you for social reasons. More importantly, executive recruiters read these periodicals.

To maintain high visibility, get your message across through the appropriate channels: publish where possible, become involved in industry functions when necessary, become community-oriented and socially active. Remember that you alone position yourself mentally and physically for that so-called "lucky break." Competence is the foundation for a fast rise, but positive visibility can hasten the trip. So think of additional methods of visibility in your chosen field as well as in your company. Keep in mind all the other companies where you could advance. If there are none, your present employer has the leverage. If there are many now, or if there are soon going to be many, you have the edge.

Remember, the president can afford the luxury of being modest. Most unassuming middle managers are left with their modesty, which too often turns to sour disappointment. They play out the frustrating role of corporate best man instead of the happy role of bridegroom.

SIZING UP SUPERIORS

5

Few middle managers ever fully analyze their many random thoughts about their current bosses. Usually, the boss is analyzed only when a crisis arises. Then he most often is viewed in a negative light because the lower level manager's reaction is subjective and defensive.

Consider the following: The conference has just ended. Clutching his sheaf of papers, Harry comes out of the smoke-filled room and scurries back to his office on a lower floor. On the way down in the elevator he muses: "What the hell did he mean when he said that we had to up production? I told him that we would run into the very problem he mentioned." Harry has just finished giving the boss a spoken catalog of rationalizations as to why a particular project is snafued. He is probably furious for being defensive, and also is in the process of convincing himself that the boss was just being cold-hearted when he subjected him to a grilling in front of all the other department heads at the meeting. By the time Harry gets back to his office and makes his first telephone call, he has justified his anger and slipped the boss into a convenient category marked "S.O.B."

The process described above is common among supervisory personnel. It occurs when managers fail to objectify a superior, so that his moves and actions can be anticipated. Instead of actively pursuing job-related, self-imposed goals, dead-end supervisors merely react to job and surroundings. Often, they have a distorted view of the boss only because it is compatible with their tenaciously held, preconceived notions.

The Martyr and the Milquetoast

This type of passive and defensive gentleman might be called the martyr manager. You've all seen him. He's the fellow who always has orders or deadlines thrust upon him by an unreasonable boss. He is the constant victim of the arbitrariness of his immediate commander, who is an unfeeling boor. Sometimes he is even affected by an executive two or three levels removed from him. His verbal style revolves around mumblings of "Wouldn't you know it, they expect me to do the whole job by next Groundhog Day," or "They're so unreasonable, but they're the bosses, I'm just a hired hand." The martyr plays the poor downtrodden underling who has no power but many just grievances. He is constantly looking for the sympathy of his subordinates.

The failure to objectify deprives the executive of another tool for success: anticipation. For if he fritters away time in constant handwringing over what the boss has just said to him at a meeting, he will never be able to spend time constructively thinking of what the boss is likely to require next. Most top executives have an ability to stop trouble before it occurs. A good anticipatory sense comes from past experience, but it is sharpened by the practice of remaining alert to what is happening in the present and by an ability to concentrate on what is about to happen.

Then there are the Caspar Milquetoast types. They are the fellows who have another sort of reaction in a conference room with the boss—they tend to passively go along with him, exuding an aura of "I'm just a dumb little boy." The little boy accepts everything the boss says, rarely displaying his feelings openly. Yet occasionally those feelings show—sometimes in a look or an offhand remark, but usually in a controlled anger that surfaces in after-hours conversation when he feels comfortable because he is surrounded by "friendlies." Here is another type who is so busy reacting that he has no time for positive anticipatory action.

It is very difficult to keep your mental dossier free of highly subjective notes. But try to judge the boss by his behavior, not by his appearance or by any grade-school stereotype. Bosses come in all shapes, sizes, and assortments.

Is Your Boss Permissive or Authoritarian?

The martyr and the Milquetoast are saddled with a common difficulty, an adverse reaction to authority. But they're only one aspect of the problem. No chapter on sizing up superiors would be complete without a brief discussion of what might be called the authority syndrome. Why do so many subordinates stay in job ruts? Is it simply because of an irrational fear of authority? Most would vigorously deny any deep-seated dependent need for an authority figure, but in fact they have one. The need has its roots in attitudes and behavior patterns adopted to cope with the dominant authority in early childhood.

Many a man finds himself in a corporate position when he has had only limited experience in coming to terms with authority. He has not yet learned to understand clearly what sort of man the boss is, and tends to fit him into a comfortable mold—the strict disciplinarian, the permissive libertarian who has not set limits, the man who pushes competitiveness and achievement at the expense of all other satisfactions. But the boss is usually far too complex for such convenient pigeonholing.

While the authority syndrome involves superiors as well as subordinates, its manifestations in the former are less evident. After all, most superiors have learned to hide their innermost feelings from subordinates. Yet a careful observation of your boss's behavior with *his* boss should yield some clues as to how he feels about authority and how he reacts to it. If he is a strict authoritarian with you, the chances are that he reacts to his superiors in strict obedience.

The authoritarian is more easily spotted than the permissive, the man who fears authority and tends not to rule firmly—in the mistaken hope that his subordinates will somehow do what he wants and will always think well of him. Most permissives fail to inspire confidence in their command, and the end result is lack of direction and achievement. Any topnotch executive will readily admit that he has made enemies —but the permissive is too concerned with popularity to hurt anyone's feelings.

The authoritarian boss demonstrates inflexibility in his every action. He is a man who does not make exceptions, lives by all the most absurd rules, criticizes people for what they look like and not how they produce, and is a stickler for detail. He is almost obsessive about never leaving any area open to discussion because he still quakes over the thought of any criticism from those in authority. It should be reassuring to young executives to realize that most overt authoritarians stamp themselves as such in a very short time. Their superiors can't help but recognize their inflexible attitudes and their inability to adapt to the subtle methods of political infighting so necessary in the upper echelons of the company.

So, don't fret over the authoritarian—he is usually pegged early in his career. If you find yourself under one of them, it may be in your favor because you probably will leapfrog him quite rapidly.

The more difficult case of authority syndrome is the permissive boss. He either has trouble setting goals or deliberately does not set them, so that his subordinates are kept in a state of confusion and doubt. This type of superior can be very harmful early in a career because the damage suffered may be irreparable to an inexperienced young executive. A young man may be led to constantly doubt his perceptions. He may never shake off the effects of breaking in under a man who keeps him off guard and who does not set clear goals.

Know Your Boss

The most helpful role of a boss is as a teacher, not in the old restrictive role of authority figure, but as someone who can help you learn what is needed to move on. So if possible, avoid making your own worst dreams come true and try to see him as he is, not as a father whose muscles seem larger than everyone else's.

When you grew you began to see your father as a man like any other man, and you should do the same thing with your boss.

To learn from a boss, one must adjust to him. Above all, one must almost never challenge his self-image.

If an insecure boss finds himself challenged in what he perceives as an unfriendly manner, he can retaliate in any number of ways to end your career with that company. If you are designated as a troublemaker, the reputation will be hard to shake. A troublemaker tag is usually used to justify firing an employee who has a high irritation factor. In a sophisticated company the troublemaker's dossier usually contains the epitaph: "He could not relate to fellow workers."

But how does one determine what a boss's self-image is? Since there may not be many opportunities to talk with and get to know a boss, most sharp juniors learn how to observe. Try to observe the man both in the office and in outside social situations. Above all, listen to what he says to you, to others in the office, to his superiors, and even to his wife. Note the most obvious traits. If he is an early arriver at the office, you had better be prepared to at least match him.

The age of a superior can be important. If he is an older man and reflects a fearfulness of the younger generation in manner and speech, he may be fearful of being replaced by a younger and perhaps more energetic man. If he is a younger man and fairly new on his job, he may still be shaky about being in a new position. If he is younger than you, he may have a problem in dealing with the authority syndrome. If it is a woman, she may feel threatened by men and be correspondingly jealous of her position. These are all possibilities that the subordinate may encounter and that he should notice.

One of the best ways to discover how the boss thinks is to explore areas of mutual compatibility. Even if you just chat about the professional football results on Monday morning, you establish rapport. A word of caution: Almost anyone can distinguish between false and genuine interest in a subject he knows something about. Stay away from forced expressions of interest in such topics as glassblowing or curling or any other esoteric subject that you might not have a genuine curiosity about. Insincerity can be self-defeating.

Keep in mind that you must perceive the boss as he really is, not as you would like him to be, or as you expect him to be, or as he appears but really isn't. Behavior does not take place in a vacuum, but rather is a response to something or someone other than yourself. In other words, you react to your boss and he to you. It's to be hoped it is a pleasant reaction, but if he stirs some unpleasant memory embedded in your psyche or if you have the same effect on him, the response may be negative. And there are all kinds of responses, verbal and nonverbal.

Nonverbal gestures can tip off a person's true feelings. Fidgeting in an interview and making distracting physical movements while talking are obvious examples, but other, more subtle gestures can be just as revealing—frowns and grimaces, for instance. People are more adept at picking up nonverbal indications of pleasure, which are reassuring, than indications of displeasure, which are disturbing.

The insightful leader must always be able to recognize the difference between what a person says and what he really feels. A man who has just been shifted to a new job in the factory may respond positively in words, but his gestures or subsequent behavior on the

68

job or with his peers may indicate that he is distressed. Many managers who have had to inform a man of an imminent job switch seldom see that the transferee is unhappy. The reason they don't is that they are too relieved about completing the transfer to worry about any dislocated feelings.

Don't Dismiss the Incompetent Boss

If you're interested in your boss's position and are always saying to your cronies that "Once I get that job, I'll understand my men and will be aware of what they want," learn from your current master. A number of top executives have told me that they learned a great deal from poor bosses they encountered early in their careers because the experience alerted them to a myriad of mistake possibilities. Observing a bad boss in action is one way to avoid having to learn from your own experience.

Not to be obnoxiously conspicuous around your boss will take some self-restraint. As improbable as it may seem, remember that the boss *can* be right. It is amazing how many ambitious men assume that he is always wrong. In any case, if the boss feels that you are contemptuous of him, he is certain not to help you advance. If you were fortunate enough to be able to attend a top business school, avoid flaunting the fact in front of a supervisor who may have worked his way up from the ranks and who may resent Harvard Business School types offering fancy theories.

As part of being the engaging learner, never challenge a boss on his terms (if possible). Avoid confrontations in his strong areas. For example, if he is an expert in labor relations, tread lightly in discussions of policy. If you must challenge him in his bailiwick, be positive of your argument and be prepared to respond to questions. Above all, do not interrupt his work in order to confront him, because you are at a disadvantage before you open your mouth. Select a more propitious time for the confrontation—perhaps a more relaxed atmosphere away from the office, because offices have a formalizing effect on free discussion. Buttonholing a man after a meeting or at the water cooler may be a more relaxed way of initiating a chat.

It is best to avoid confrontations over policy unless you have built a relationship that can stand the strain of total honesty. This is quite rare in the business world, but it is possible. Better to broach the topic by saying something like, "Why don't we review our position on this policy?" rather than the negative and somewhat hostile, "You know, I think that you are wrong to implement this policy this way."

Know Your Place

Since there is no doubt in the business world as to the validity of the old saw that discretion is the better part of valor, the junior man should always be available at the request of the senior man. Yet perhaps a little fudging is acceptable. For instance, if the boss peers into your office at 9:30 and says he would like to see you, there may be some point in saying that there are a few little items that you have to clear up before you can join him. Since most bosses end their request for your presence with an offhand "—when you have a chance," you can usually take your time. Of course, it would be well to consider the tone of the remark. If there is an urgency in it, make yourself available immediately.

Rarely is a man dropped solely for not using the

right or preferred lines of communication in a company —but it can be a factor. Suppose the boss is a former Army or Navy officer. If he has served for any substantial length of time, it would be reasonable to assume that he abides by the rigid practice of the chain of command, a dominant feature of any hierarchy. He does not appreciate a subordinate who "goes over his head," and he usually notes who makes correct use of the chain of command.

If you plan to go over your boss on the table of organization, let him know about it beforehand. This can be accomplished by sending him a carbon of a memo or by simply telling him. If he objects, you can always drop the idea.

People adapt to the situations that they find themselves in and since most business hierarchies are either well-defined by assorted charts and tables, or undefined, but functioning according to unwritten rules and behavior patterns, the executive who is promotable tends toward the style he finds inherent in the structure. If you are currently perched somewhere on the lower rungs of the ladder, hold in check any strong tendency to authoritarianism, because those above you will spot it immediately. The subtle or not-so-subtle use of authority comes into play at higher levels of management.

How to Get an Idea Across

What about a boss's coolness to suggestions? "But he always rejects my ideas." A statement like that indicates a proclivity to hangdogism. You've all seen the look, it usually appears after a proposal has been rejected or put off. But instead of playing the rejected lover, try to gather more facts about why the boss has turned down an idea. In other words, if you are going to be a top executive, start practicing overall planning and company policy and stop clinging to a parochial view.

Let's illustrate. Assume that you are working for a privately held company. In a meeting or in a published statement of policy the president has indicated that the firm wishes to "go public."

From that statement, one knows that the management of the company seeks spectacular short-term sales results to impress the stock-buying public. The goal may be achieved by concentration on certain ongoing projects and by putting a "hold" on other projects that might in the long run be very profitable, but that would involve a large initial drain on present earnings.

The practice of playing policy on paper, or "Here is what I would have done," can be beneficial. For one thing, you can play the game of managing your company secretly, all the while checking your recommendations against the solutions prescribed by management. For another, you never lose, and chances are that you will learn something about the way the company management thinks and comes to decisions.

Respect for a boss's attitudes can be difficult. Henry Ford, for example, did not want to be known by his subordinates. So keep your distance from the man who prefers to be an enigma. Don't pressure him by saying: "Have you gotten around to that memo yet?" Chances are you may never like the boss, but do learn to respect his wishes. And above all, learn to conceal any hostility you have for him. Again, gestures can show the perceptive boss exactly how you feel toward him. When you feel your anger creeping up to the spillover point, some sort of separation may be in order. If a three-day weekend isn't possible, a visit to another department or to the water cooler may soften your perspective.

If you do have a problem curbing a tendency to fume and fuss, try to channel your energies positively. Focus on aspects of the job that the boss has no control over and try to look over him to the next assignment.

However, do not miscalculate his intentions—as did the production man who at meetings would always talk about cost-cutting, assuming that his boss was interested only in saving money. He was wrong. The boss had said that he did not want quality sacrificed for price, but the production man cynically chose to reject the boss's statement. Eventually the man was transferred to another department where he had no contact with the boss.

When in doubt, accept your superior's statement at face value. If he puts it in written form, you can always fall back on the memo as proof of what he wanted.

What about the boss who does not put orders into memo form and when some project falls through, blames the subordinate and claims that he never issued any such order? One way to handle this problem: double-check the order with him when he issues it. That way, it is straight in your mind and it is reinforced in his. He knows that you have checked it and that both of you are now clear on the intent. As a result, he might be a little reluctant to renege on the order later. If he gives an order to you in a meeting, write it down. If he sees you writing it down, he will remember and pause when he tries to switch edicts. You can also take notes and offer him a retyped version, for verification or for his files. That way you have a permanent record of his thoughts.

What about the man who is fond of cutting costs on plans submitted to him and then criticizes the finished product? In some cases, the executive has so many other projects going that he does not remember the details of your pet project. In that case be a bit indulgent.

Don't Downgrade Yourself

Your ability to see exactly where the boss stands in the company power structure is important to the campaign that you wage to promote yourself. Is he going up, or is he merely tolerated at this stage of his career? It is possible to work for a man who is not going to advance (for any number of reasons) but who may still have limited power because of an ability to offer good ideas or because of strong technical skills.

But no boss—be he a man on the way up, or a man who knows that he has reached his plateau—will admire or promote a subordinate who shows low self-esteem. A poor self-image can be shown in a myriad of ways: from badmouthing one's own projects, to extreme defensiveness in all areas of the job, to lack of sustained drive on a project. Self-esteem can be determined by the way a person carries himself or in the way he dresses. On the other hand, people with low self-esteem can also cover deficiencies with a swaggering manner. They have all the answers.

Taking over a boss's job has always been associated with backstabbing. While this may be the case in isolated instances, it is not true in the large majority of promotions. The old adage ''You can catch more flies with honey than with vinegar'' applies to the corporate scramble for power. Being supportive in an organization will most often lead to advancement. And don't falsely assume that sincere support of the boss is apple polishing.

Not many people like to assume responsibility for a supervisor's mistakes, but if you can do so tactfully, he will appreciate your gesture. However, do not overdo it, because a number of bosses take advantage of generosity and tend to lay all their mistakes on a willing fall guy.

Should You Be Outspoken?

When do you speak out? The answer quite frankly is: almost never. But it depends on the company and your boss. There is no hard and fast rule on this point, but there are a number of taboos.

For example, do not send him too many memos or notes on your favorite brainstorms—especially if a word in private would do. Do not saddle him with too many decisions and do not put him in the position of having to constantly turn down your ideas. Do not put him on the spot, even to make the point that you were right about a decision or policy. Forget the tendency to say "I told you so." Think before you speak. In fact, you would do well if you can help him think that your idea came from him. Save your hard sell for someone else.

One of the most agreeable assets a subordinate can have is a willingness to perform tasks distasteful to the boss. How does one tell what is distasteful to him? By noting what he avoids doing on the job. It could be speaking to a secretary about chores, it could be completing an important memo, it could be remembering a production deadline. The most important thing is the way you offer your help. In the case of a memo, you could tell him something like "I've been thinking about the new plant and have jotted down a few notes you might want to include in your interoffice memo." That way he feels that he will include your suggestion in *his memo.*

Help your boss clarify his thinking. This can be accomplished by role-playing with him. The conversation could begin: "What do you plan to say to Snavely this afternoon in his office? I think our tack should be that we want the new man, but we would like to meet with him to explain our procedures. How does that sound, Al?"

If your boss forwards an idea to you and then says "Run with it," don't begin asking him about a great many details. Details are your job. He doesn't care how you do it as long as you get it done.

If you have come from a rival firm or another company in another industry, don't remind the boss how you did things at good old XYZ corporation. Trumpeting another company's methods is usually like waving a red flag in front of the man who hired you away. The exception, of course, is if you were brought in specifically for your knowledge of your former company.

Don't push for an answer from the boss on a project that demands a decision if it is to keep rolling. He usually is well aware that you are waiting—so stay away from him and let him approach you with his decision. If you must have a decision, try to talk to him about another aspect of the project, one that would perhaps serve to remind him of the current problem.

WORKING WITH SUBORDINATES

6

Why do some middle managers fail when they are appointed to top positions? Why do others succeed brilliantly and soon move to higher levels of managerial responsibility?

This chapter deals with the reasons why some men cope and others do not when the ''big chance'' arises. After discussing some of the major problems that surface when a man is named to a new job, we will consider ways of dealing with subordinates so as to increase the chances of being promoted.

Managers fail for a variety of reasons, but one of the most striking, and the one that can be linked to almost all other problems, is what might be termed ''postponed learning disease.'' The earliest symptoms of this common executive illness occur at the lowest supervisory levels and can become acute by the time a man moves into the upper echelons. The illness manifests itself in the following manner.

Jack has just been promoted. He is so happy with his new position of power that he is not thinking ahead to the day when he moves to the next higher position. After two or three jumps on the organization chart, he finds himself saying: "This authority and responsibility is not as hard to deal with as I thought." He stops listening to and learning about the new problems that confront him. He begins to rely on solutions that worked on a lower level. One day, he is suddenly propelled into a top echelon spot. He is lost. He has not prepared for the job, and so he either panics, or is ground down by the increased competition from shrewder fellow executives.

Learn from Your Subordinates

When job paralysis sets in, it is usually because an executive has not built a solid foundation of managerial experience. The result is a man who spends the rest of his corporate career trying to adjust to a new position, or who looks forward to retirement, or who shudderingly awaits the inevitable pink slip. Moral: You might as well learn the refinements of leadership on the way to the top. The inoculation for postponed learning disease contains a heavy dosage of experiential learning at lower levels, with supplementary reinforcements at each subsequent level of employment.

And, strange as it may seem to many supervisors, subordinates are a strong source for learning skills that will be useful in other positions of greater authority. A supervisor can sometimes learn more from subordinates than they from him.

Just because you have reached a supervisory level does not mean that you are automatically skilled in every area. You may know technique and have the necessary formal education for a job, but you may be sadly deficient in certain departments.

In the catalog of skills, you may have some, your workers others. They may overlap, they may not. And what you value may not be as important as the skills your subordinates value. For example, they may put great stock in the ability to get along with others; you prefer a man who comes to work on time. Learn the value system of those under you.

How to Deal with Subordinates' "Hangups"

Even the appearance or outward behavior of subordinates can be deceiving and therefore not a true barometer of an ability to think and act creatively. Some may appear nervous or shy in your presence, but are competent and cool in tight situations. Others may give no outward sign of being able to meet goals, but can efficiently do so. Some have a hard time expressing themselves in front of an audience. If you encounter this type, perhaps the best approach is to discuss with him what he is about to present before he goes into a meeting. In that way, you can assure him of your support for his project and at the same time give him an opportunity to preview what he plans to present to the audience. Reinforcement for a subordinate will enable him to do a better job and be less fearful of the next goal that you set for him or that he sets for himself.

But be skeptical of the well-put-together man in your office, the one who says that he can handle any type of assignment that you toss him. He may well be able to do a first-rate job, but all too often an underling who asks no questions and proclaims loud and clear that he is able to master a new project with little or no effort is simply covering up nervous apprehension. He is usually the type who, because of insecurity about his ability to learn or produce, never says that he might have trouble with an assignment. He can do anything. But what happens? He frets and worries about the impending deadline on the project and is afraid to seek the help that he probably needs to complete it satisfactorily. Don't let a subordinate's paralysis snafu a project whose ultimate success or failure will reflect on your managerial ability.

If a subordinate shows signs of paralysis before the project is due or finished, reassign it. When you do so, however, be careful to take the project away without either reproaching the man or making him feel that he has deeply disappointed you. Don't make him believe that he is totally incompetent and unable to function. This will only create resentment and anger, which could be detrimental to other workers and future projects. One way to salve his ego would be to assign him to another project. You could also tell him that the new project takes precedence over the one he has been working on. Allow the man a way to rationalize his failure and at the same time show him you have confidence in him.

One of the most competent men I ever knew could not articulately present his thoughts in a meeting, but privately he was clear on almost every phase of a project. More importantly, he could complete the job in the manner he said he would. His hesitation and shyness in a meeting had to be overlooked, for the man knew how to produce.

I know of many company presidents who cannot "relate to the men" as well as immediate supervisors can. But every topnotcher realizes that he cannot know everything and deals with this self-knowledge objectively—usually by mastering the skill of delegating. The first requisite for delegating is trust, a trust that comes from your own security about the job and your ability to learn what is necessary to master it.

Adjustment to a New Situation

Before we discuss adjustment problems on a new job, it may be pertinent to mention the social aspects. Let's say that Joe has just been promoted out of the group that he has been a part of since he entered the company training program. Aware that some of his "classmates" would be promoted more rapidly than others—once the initial winnowing process has taken place—Joe has already learned to cope with the unhappy situation of trying to be friendly with men who are potential rivals for the top positions in the company. At any rate, Joe has been promoted. In addition to restructuring his relationships with his classmates (especially if he is now someone's direct superior) he must adjust not only to a new group of subordinates but to the executives above him, who now probably begin to accept him while realizing he is a potential threat to their security.

If Joe had come into a new company and not been part of a rising group, the problems of human adjustment would not be so acute. But there would be other adjustment problems, such as fitting into a completely new company with all its taboos and unwritten rules.

As Joe moves up, the new people around him will see him in a new light and expect him to play his appointed role according to the rules of the firm. Joe may not feel any different, but he must be aware that he is now in a position to exert control over some former peers, and that they will necessarily regard him in a new way.

If you have been promoted, forget about the man you have replaced. Even if you are constantly reminded by his former secretary about the way he performed on the job, try to ignore his methodology—especially if he was fired. If your predecessor was promoted, make his job over in your image by taking the best of what he did and mixing well with your own abilities. Good men define assignments and rarely are put off by job descriptions, which are by definition restrictive and usually outdated by the time they are mimeographed.

Recognize Value Differences

It is a truism that money equals status in the United States—but fortunately, there are exceptions. Those who do not have money, and have little chance of ever accumulating a great sum of it, manage to invent their own value systems and hold pretty rigidly to them. Status is truly in the eye of the beholder. If a group that you belong to does not share your system, it might as well not exist.

Let us illustrate the importance of correctly perceiving the value system in which you operate. One of the chief problems for companies that send executives abroad continues to be the clash between the habits and attitudes of the freshly scrubbed, ready-to-go executives and the habits and attitudes of the people they come in contact with.

Very often, the ugly American does not know he acts like an ugly American. In the Middle East one does not give a person something with the left hand, because the left hand is considered unclean. Each country has its own peculiarities. Few forget the Eskimo practice of having the visitor sleep with the host's wife. If the guest declines, he is considered rude. Most customs are not that extreme, but the feelings they evoke can be intensely real.

Understanding the value system in which you operate is just as important in dealing with subordinates as it is in dealing with people in foreign countries. Respect is not a one-way operation: Respect your subordinates and chances are that they will respect you in return.

The Art of Delegating

As you ascend the ladder, even more interpersonal competence is needed because the higher up you go, the more involved in people problems you find yourself. At higher corporate levels you have experts working for you in a number of technical areas, so your main function is problem solving in the area of staff personality.

One of the major reasons why you have to begin to delegate authority for technical details is obvious. Ask a few middle-level technicians who started their own business in "the good old days." To a man they will tell you that a major reason behind their getting less involved in the detail work was that they lacked the knowledge to cope with changes in business methods. It happens in any industry that moves ahead. The plant manager who once dealt with manual production lines is lost when faced with all the intricacies of automated equipment. The office manager very often does not understand the new generation of computers that have been installed in his bailiwick.

The gentle art of delegation is a necessary tool in the ambitious man's get-ahead kit of acquired skills.

As one rises in the company, responsibilities inevitably become greater than one's ability to handle them. The entrepreneur of the old school, who was the chief authority on everything in the company, wouldn't last in today's corporate structure, where you must delegate to survive. The problem is not whether or not to delegate, it is how to do so, and, more importantly, when.

The expert delegator can move faster than most others in an organization because he has a clear vision of what his talent can do for him. He has learned what tasks to delegate and what chores to handle himself so that he gains maximum exposure in the proper places, that is, with the men in the top power positions. Properly applied, delegation can be a vital factor in working with subordinates.

First, let's consider why an executive assigns tasks. The most important reason is because of the freedom it affords him to perform as a boss should. He can concentrate on long-range planning, can plot politically if need be, can prepare for problems he anticipates in the next few months or in the next year. It also gives him the time to take an overview of his operation and reevaluate his personal progress in the light of what he sees.

One of the best illustrations of the problem of deputizing subordinates is that of the former salesman who has just become sales manager. Let's take the case of Dave. Dave was always a crack salesman, one who really knew his territory. Now he finds himself in a new office—away from his fellow salesmen. As hard as it is to get used to the idea, he realizes that he is now their boss. Instead of merely meeting his own quotas, he must set quotas for his men. Instead of submitting travel plans and expenses, he must approve the plans and expense vouchers of others. Instead of spending a lot of time on the road in other executives' offices, he must devote the greater part of his time to organizing and implementing company sales goals for all the territories, not just his own. He must now turn from continual self-motivation to ways to motivate his "troops."

As is often the case with top salesmen who have been elevated to a management position, Dave is running into the problem of relinquishing his territory to the young man who has replaced him. He still makes it a point to go out to see old clients and even has accompanied the new man on his sales visits. If Dave had introduced his new man to his old customers and then stepped back to allow him to work out his own relationships, all would have been well (this is true in most cases, unless a sales manager deliberately chooses an inefficient replacement), but he did not. Either Dave is fearful of the responsibilities of the new job and still clings to the older, more comfortable way of doing business, or he is experiencing what might be termed the "possessive mother" syndrome. He balks at letting "his" territory be taken over by a younger man, who indeed might have a different method of selling his old customers. He frets that he will not be able to relate to the new people that he must come in contact with in his new role.

Dave obviously is a man who found the change from specialist to generalist difficult. His major problem was that he lacked the insight into his strengths and shortcomings to readily make the adjustment to delegating. Only when a man has a clear idea of his own talents can he then zero in on those others who can help him in the areas where he lacks expertise.

But if you are intent on avoiding the problems Dave

encountered, begin early. After you have determined what areas you need help in, set out to find the men who can supply that help. Do not get involved in avoiding a very talented man. If he is an expert or if he can simply do the job well, it can only reflect favorably on you for having chosen him. Never choose a man on the basis of his being less of a "threat." If a man has talent, let him use it. Don't stifle him. Utilizing a first-rate man whenever possible is a positive policy for all concerned—the company, your career, the subordinate's future. If you advance through a policy of submerging talent instead of picking the best people available, your own ability to function will suffer. Unless you demand the best people and then demand the best that's in them, you will be shortchanging both them and the company. How many times have you heard men early in a career say: "I remember old Charlie. He was a tough and demanding son-of-a-gun to work with, but when I finished, I knew my job." Pity the poor subordinates who have not been challenged, stimulated, or prodded into producing at a higher capacity. The same can be said of those who do not choose subordinates who push them to greater efforts.

Grooming a Successor Can Pay Off

One way to insure that there will be no hesitation when the bigwigs think of promoting you is to groom a replacement. If you start to operate on a lower level with the idea of making yourself irreplaceable, chances are you will stay there. But if you've prepared a capable successor, top management will be less hesitant about promoting you. In fact, there are executives (who are usually not aware of the fact) who have been promoted so that management could move up their subordinates.

One way to groom men is to rotate their assignments and hand out special ones. This practice is best exemplified on the top levels of major corporations. Here the man being groomed spends a few years at the head of various divisions and in various parts of the country. He becomes an "internationalist" within his own company.

Another way of grooming a replacement is to delegate responsibility to him. You thereby contribute positively to his self-image and on-the-job satisfaction and, as a result, you make him more productive. You also prepare him for a better position someday (and don't think that subordinates are not well aware of this important factor in their own career plans).

Be extremely careful in the matter of assignments. Do not proffer an assignment and then take it away. Do not give a subordinate a major assignment and then never again allow him to operate with as much authority. A man who has tasted independence is likely to chafe if you fail to keep him well-supplied with mind-expanding projects.

Much has been said about the need to delegate, but little about exactly how to do it. Here are a few tips. After making yourself clear as to exactly what you want and expect from the assignee, tell him what the goals are. Do *not* tell him how to do it: That is *his* job. If he expresses some hesitancy about the assignment and how to go about doing it, you can begin by saying: "Well, one way to approach it might be . . ." In that way he will leave your office with an idea of how you want to proceed and still feel that it is his idea.

Some thoughts about overtraining or overcoaching are appropriate here. The overtrained or oversupervised employee tends to be rigid and less creative. His initiative can shrink in direct proportion to the freedom that you allow him on the job. One of the reasons you have delegated a piece of company business to him is to find a fresh way of approaching a problem. If his initiative is stifled by a harsh system of rules and checks, he is not likely to surprise you with innovation. Both the company and the man lose a creative opportunity.

Make Assignments Carefully

As a supervisor, you have the responsibility of assigning the tough jobs and seeing that those assigned to handle them have the latitude to carry them out. A subordinate's growth requires the increased self-confidence that comes from coping with a tough assignment. Like the child struggling to master his physical surroundings, he must be allowed to fail and return to the task with a minimum of interference. Only in a continuously supportive atmosphere can he learn and move on to the next function or task. When my son was learning to walk, he found a little bridge in the park and proceeded to spend an hour walking over and around it. He repeated the process for what seemed to me an interminable time, until I realized that he was mastering the function of walking in a new situation. After I understood what this project meant to him, I decided that I could afford the time. His actions were not irrational. For him the project at hand—learning to walk—was serious. Now, when we return to the same little bridge in the park, he runs right over it and moves on. He has mastered the bridge and his relation to it.

To get back to subordinates and the need to assign them tasks that are not below their capabilities: Remember that a person can get a feeling of exhilaration out of doing a difficult task well—so give him the opportunity. Sometimes the subtle squelching of creativity has to do with managers who feel that they have their own "turf" to protect. Show that you feel that a man can do the job, and at the same time, make certain he knows that you are available for consultation on any of its aspects, and at any stage of his progress.

If it is to be a joint venture in a department within your jurisdiction, be sure to outline the assignment carefully in advance so as to clarify areas where there might be disagreement. At the same time, resist any tendency to direct all conversation. Do not give answers to possible problems unless you are asked. In fact, encourage subordinates to come up with the answers themselves. Do not be surprised if they do it in a way that you never would have thought of. That is how one learns from subordinates. It's the old story of "Please, Mother, I'd rather do it myself."

Try hard to avoid delegating only those tasks you find onerous. Chances are that they will be onerous to a subordinate also, and if he feels that you are just burdening him to spare yourself, he will not pursue them with any enthusiasm. Let your men handle assignments that you yourself are keen on. One method of interesting the assignee might be to state: "I would take this assignment myself, Jim, but I just don't have the time and I feel that you can probably do a great job on it. I feel that it's a plum."

How much control should you exert over a delegated task? In a word, as little as possible. For most people, "control" probably conjures up an image of an executive exercising his authority. Here I use control to mean that ability to genuinely delegate—not give naked orders. To be effective, an order must be couched in terms the subordinate can understand and it must be agreeably presented.

Support Your Subordinates

One of the overlooked problems that comes with a promotion is the social one. A middle manager is elevated to a new position and performs as if all that is required of him is the ability to do the job. He is either deliberately avoiding the social aspects of his new job, or covering up his own social deficiencies. Almost everyone who becomes a boss realizes that he must soon involve himself in the field of human relations. One of the major roles of a new superior is support of subordinates, and one must learn to refrain from supporting any action that is detrimental to either a particular person or company policy. Perhaps support can best be defined as an encouraging and validating act that furthers company policy while leading to greater satisfaction for the individuals involved. Support indicates that you are interested in the rights of others, and one of the major roles of support is to insure those rights.

Support does not mean that you must become ''one of the boys.'' You can establish managerial distance without subordinates thinking they are out of sight and that you are unreachable. At the same time, strive to avoid the ''good guy'' tag, which can be risky, because your ability to command can be undermined if the group looks upon you as a peer only, and not as a leader.

Consider Your Subordinates' Needs

If you are an adviser who coldly submits company objectives to your men without any regard for how they may feel about them, or if you fail to anticipate how they may react, you are little more than a message sender. You must communicate to them that it is in their best interest to do a particular project well. One way to motivate positively is to be clear when you accept the project from your own superior as to how it will affect the needs of your subordinates. For example, if you feel that a rush project for the company will keep various personnel working overtime, you should communicate that fact to the upper level. When you explain this to your superior, after mentally working out how you think the people under you will react, he will more than likely accept your job estimate. He will also be aware that you are keeping in mind the best interests of your men. When you do announce the project, you will have removed a possible obstacle to its completion.

In other words, if you know that Kate Jones cannot work overtime Tuesday, Wednesday, and Friday because she is attending a local college and taking courses that are very important to her, you have in a sense worked out in advance an alternative plan so that she can attend these classes and not feel pressured into working on this project at the expense of her outside education. When you discuss the project with her, begin by saying something like: "Kate, I know you have classes Tuesday, Wednesday, and Friday, so I have asked Miss Smith to fill in for you then. We won't need you at that time." As a result of this thoughtfulness, Kate Jones will probably do a good job for you in the hours that she does work on the project. You have been aware of and communicated your needs (that is, your subordinates' needs) to your superiors and managed to launch a project auspiciously. Nor has company policy suffered. You have supported both your subordinates and your company—the best possible combination for growth.

Find the Group Leader

One of the problems with support is that it is sometimes difficult to find the person in a group of people working under you who can best communicate what you want from the group. This man or woman is a group leader. He is the man that you will have to convince in order to get the work done. Since sociologists and psychologists have concluded that there are formal leaders and informal group leaders, it is important to discuss the difference. By formal leader I mean a man who by his job description and very position appears to be the man in charge. However, very often in a group there is a man who is the informal group leader. He is the one people go to for advice and help with their decision making, very often bypassing the formal, or titled leader.

Just how does one spot the real leader? Suppose you have been assigned to a new plant and are in the process of getting to know your new workers. You have a formal chart in front of you, but that does not indicate the man or woman who you have to reach.

You can notice a leader by the tenor of discussions that other people have around him. If he seems available and is quite often seen chatting or conferring with any number of people in the group, he may be your man. He may become the informal spokesman of the group, or may take it upon himself to introduce you to the people in the office or to office procedures. Very often he can handle himself around people in a work situation quite well.

One of the best ways to spot an informal leader is to watch the traffic to his office (if he has one). Very often there is a constant shuffling of people in and out. If his immediate superior continually seeks him out, instead of the other way around, most likely he is the informal group leader.

In addition to the group leader there are other, potential, leaders. A "potential" is not threatened by your presence and can help you mobilize his peers to cope with a particular job.

There are a number of ways to spot the potential leader. He volunteers: He is the man who is ready to assume new responsibilities. But do not measure him by the number of tasks he is willing to take on. Rather, judge him by what he does when you give him a task after he volunteers for it. If he does well, increase his burden of responsibilities. But in the beginning make sure that the tasks you assign do not overtax his ability. Otherwise he will be discouraged and not readily volunteer the next time.

There are many other ways to spot the "potential." Usually he has an uncanny knack of using his available resources to solve a problem. Very rarely does he return for help, and he is very clear on the assignment the moment you give it to him. If he does not know the answer himself he knows how to marshal the appropriate resources so as to find it without bothering you. He very rarely panics. He is *not* the man who has a head full of facts but cannot sort them out. He does not pick the right answer at the wrong time. He is flexible and can handle an assignment that calls for many changes in perception and differing approaches. You can be certain he will seek all avenues and options before he gives up on an assignment. He has the ability to meet deadlines. Most probably you will not receive from him a series of memos dealing with a number of unanticipated delays.

He will also relish handling pertinent detail. The subordinate who likes to delegate unnecessarily and who avoids detail work may in fact be a shirker, or a person who sets up scapegoats so that he can fob off his own mistakes.

The potential leader rarely presents problems; instead, he offers solutions. Yet he leaves the solution to your discretion, knowing that you usually have more information about the project than he does. Thus, when a subordinate comes knocking at your door seeking an audience and then presents a problem, ask him if he has any ideas about a solution. If he ordinarily has no idea of how to solve a problem, he is probably not leadership material. Any man who has not thought about a practical way to solve a problem should not have come in crying about it to a superior.

A "potential," on the other hand, always keeps his facts in order. If he puts something in a memo or outlines a presentation for you there is very little chance that he has not checked his sources or failed to do his research.

Nor does the potential leader inundate you with accounts of his achievements or with memos pointing out what a great job he has done. He is a doer; he is less concerned with appearance than with results. Even if he seems rough around the edges, do not discourage him from presenting data as he sees it. Your job as his superior is to make the best use of the raw material that he supplies.

Of major importance in evaluating a "potential" is his discouragement factor. If he becomes discouraged at every slight problem in the project you assign him, watch out. While you may occasionally have to encourage the potential leader or spend time helping him over his nervousness, he usually does not need a superior's paternalistic or obviously supportive reassurances. He feels secure in the knowledge that he can do a job, and will respect you more if you treat him as a person who can do it than if you act like a father who is passing out an assignment to test him. And he has the flexibility needed to surmount the unforeseen problems that may arise.

Last but not least, he has the inner security to admit to having made a mistake. He does not spend precious time hiding a blunder; he simply acknowledges it and continues with his work.

How to Listen

It is easy to talk about respect for a subordinate, another thing to practice it. As the old railroad crossing signs advised—stop, look, and listen. Above all, you must be a good listener, and at the same time you must develop the ability to respond directly to what a person is saying to you. In other words, the chief requisite is empathy. Avoid listening to gossip. If a subordinate knows that he cannot gossip with you he will feel that you are not interested in another person's talk about him. Mutual trust is then established.

There is a vast difference between being a father confessor and being a good listener. The father confessor routine should be played down or avoided altogether because it can take up too much time. It can also lead to resentment among subordinates if they feel you are spending too much time with a person who has "problems." In addition, you risk alienating an insecure superior. He may feel that you communicate much better with subordinates than with him.

One element usually forgotten by many superiors: Listen to a subordinate even if you know the answer to his problem. But encourage him to arrive at a solution himself, because he will thereby derive greater satisfaction than if you had provided it.

One of the best ways to help a subordinate is to role-play with him. Just say something like: "Well, why don't I pretend that I am you, and you take my part?" In that way, he will be more comfortable speaking with you. You might also learn from the experience.

Respect Fosters Respect

A fine way to show respect for a subordinate is to offer him a participating role. Have him consult with you on selective matters open to discussion (matters that do not compromise company policy or "top secret" information). This makes him feel he is not just an unnoticed cog in the corporate machine. Yet while most subordinates appreciate a chance to participate, heavily dependent people often resent the freedom offered them and actually prefer authority. Be careful, because individual situations often define the use of the shared, or participatory, role.

It is important to show your personal interest in your subordinates by providing them with information about their job and the company. That is done well by most thinking managers. But many managers remain reluctant to share personal events with lower echelon personnel. This is a mistake, because if a worker sees only a "superior" boss, he will not see a "human" boss. Nor will he feel that he and his boss are cooperating on a venture as teammates. A clever, popular politician like the late Mayor Curley of Boston recognized the appeal of being human and open—to such an extent, in fact, that he was reelected while in jail. The old theory that a manager should restrict information about himself should not be rigorously adhered to. What a man doesn't know he fears. When he knows a little about you, he can identify; he can feel compatibility; he can build empathy. Without information he is incapable of understanding or feeling that you are just like him in many ways. If he knows nothing, there is no shared experience to build on. Most "cold fish" bosses receive adequate production and no more.

A good supervisor has to develop the ability to want to know his men. There may be a man who "puts you off" or "gives you the creeps," but you must abandon initial visceral feelings. Accept him for what he is. If you do, and make an honest effort to treat him the way you would like to be treated, it can help immeasurably. Accept the view that people can change. If you feel that a man is not capable of change or growth or a desire to achieve greater satisfaction, all your supportive efforts will seem phony to him because you will not be supporting him with any degree of confidence. Yet if you become more open with a subordinate and in the process help him drop some of his own defenses, you will be a better leader.

Another way to respect a subordinate: Give him credit for accomplishments. How you do it and publicize it is crucial. Never take credit for a subordinate's ideas or achievements. The best way to publicize him and yourself is through a memo. The memo might begin: "My fellow worker Tom Johnson came up with the idea that . . ." After you have inserted a subordinate's name in a memo headed for your superior, give the subordinate a blind copy. That way, the boss knows that you give credit where credit is due and the subordinate knows that you care about your men. One of the worst mistakes a budding top executive can make is to accept the praise for work that has been done by his subordinates. Eventually, resentful subordinates will stunt any further chances for cooperative efforts, thus slowing your upward mobility. Also, one day your superior might talk to a subordinate and find out that you appropriated his idea and claimed it as your own.

Respect your subordinates by not promising what you can't deliver. If a man decides that you make promises that you cannot keep, he will not approach you. He will not confide in you and you will lose a potential source of information. If someone makes a request, it is best to tell him that you would like to think about it. In that way, he will feel that you are taking the time to carefully consider it. More importantly, it allows you time to think of all the possibilities and to come up with the right answer.

By gaining the respect of subordinates, you lessen the chances that they will undercut you or, worst of all, not make themselves available to help you. The extra aid that they can offer can be important in a pinch. Suppose that you are under pressure to quickly finish a particular project for a superior. If you need overtime help from a secretary or another man to complete the job and have not built rapport with them, it is not likely that they will strain or sacrifice free time to help you. You will discover that the secretary leaves at precisely five o'clock, and that the man you counted on is too busy with other projects. On the other hand, a subordinate who respects you, and a secretary who really wants to help, can always find time.

How to Deal with Problem People

One of the most common problems facing an executive is that of dealing with ''problem'' people. Your ability to handle these people with diplomatic skill can often lead to a call to higher echelon service. There are many varieties of problem people, and one or more is liable to pop up in any work situation.

Let's discuss a few of the more common types. What do you do about the man who is intoxicated by work? The more he labors, the higher he gets. He is addicted. In some cases, he may work long hours into the night worrying over minor details, and he will always insist that he must put in overtime. Often the man is avoiding other life situations. It may be his family; it may be a particular personal problem that he has not been able to face; it may be dread of a project in the office. It is up to you to break the pattern by trying to root out what the man feels is blocking him. If possible, gently break his routine and also impress upon him that he will be able to do a better job if he talks about why he is avoiding situations by his obsession with petty work detail. Very often, a chat with the work addict's friends can help. Caution: you are not the company psychiatrist. Do not attempt to play the difficult role of amateur psychology expert. If necessary, suggest that the man seek company help (if available) or outside consultation.

Many corporations still assume that they must constantly pit employees against each other in order to spur production at both the individual and corporate level. The myth persists: There are many top corporations in which one finds the unhappy situation of executives battling fellow executives for a larger piece of the action or the president's attention, while neglecting the true focus of competition, namely to outdo a rival company. Some people respond positively to encounter management, but most do not. Some people have extensive experience with it, but their espousal of it does not necessarily mean it works. A department strategy that pits one salesman against another (not in a sales competition) and that encourages personality conflict and constant pushing by superiors will become counterproductive: The tone and morale of the department will suffer.

What About Encounter Management?

One of the major ways to avoid encounter management is to direct the energy of your department at beating the competition. Compete against your competitors, not against yourselves. Instead of constantly lining up your products for review and evaluation, thereby getting your workers overly concerned about internal criticisms, seek ways that you can improve your own products so as to outsell the competition.

Some business pundits suspect that the man who most encourages encounter management is a boss on a level "above the crowd." He cannot be hurt by any conflict and takes a somewhat sadistic pleasure in watching his underlings fight either for his favor or for a higher spot in the company. Such a man fails to realize that he not only damages the overall effectiveness of a department but creates a negative impression of his leadership with the people above him. As a long-term policy, encounter management is restrictive and injurious to growth—for both the company and its workers.

After all is said and done about subordinates, the fact is that you as a boss need them. You must therefore be able to see them as they are and anticipate how they will react in a work situation: You must be able to objectively interpret their interpersonal competence. Your ability to handle personality conflicts, for example, can make the difference between a positive and negative work atmosphere. After all, managing is the art of changing relationships to produce a growth pattern. It's what enables a company to reach its goal and its personnel to find satisfaction. Forget the manual on being a boss. Each situation is unique and you must adjust accordingly.

This chapter hopefully offered alternatives to a few of the great shibboleths of management with regard to ''handling'' subordinates. It tried to show that one does *not* handle them. They are learning partners, and you will not be less of a leader for acknowledging that they can help you. It is possible to be personal with subordinates and still be an effective boss.

GETTING THE MOST OUT OF THE BOONDOCKS

7

Every man who wants to get ahead in a corporation shudders at the thought of being assigned to some remote corporation outpost in the so-called boondocks. He knows that once there he will no longer have access to the people in power, the people he must reach to further his chances for corporate glory.

Most people think of the boondocks as small towns where the sidewalks are rolled in at nine in the evening, where there is no bus service, and where any social life revolves around the local bowling alley or cocktail lounge. But in truth, an executive can be in a boondock in a large city—even New York, Chicago, or Los Angeles—if the corporation's nerve center is elsewhere.

I once placed a call to the New York City sales office of a corporation whose headquarters was in a small Indiana town. The man who answered the phone was more than happy to provide me with the name of the appropriate person to talk with at headquarters. After much effusive and ingratiating palaver, he stated his real purpose. Would I mention his name, or the fact that I had received the upper echelon man's name from him? In that way, he could make his point with superiors at headquarters.

This is one way of maintaining a high profile in a regional office—even a big city regional office. However, suppose that I had had a negative reason for wanting to talk with the man at headquarters. In that case, the gentleman in New York would have made a serious mistake. If you are laboring in a regional or out-of-the-way location away from the man you are trying to impress, make sure that the caller who will relay your message has a positive reason for reaching your superior. In other words, make the man state his purpose and then try to determine whether it's positive or negative. You're not going to score with the superior in the home office if you refer a man to him he does not want to speak with. Your superior in the home office counts on you to screen unpleasant people, and feels it's part of your job as his subordinate.

That was an example of one way to gain attention from higher-ups not in your immediate vicinity. But what can you do if you feel that you have been assigned to an out-of-the-way location? What is the quickest way to return to the home office, where visibility is high and where you can deal directly with your competitors? The answer is that you can either consider yourself isolated and view the "boys" in the main office as all against you and unapproachable, or you can set about the task before you in such a way as to make the decision makers back at company headquarters ask: Who is that man in XYZ region?

Establish Your Identity

While you are in the boondocks, make yourself highly visible. If you do, don't worry, because word of your presence will reach the head office soon enough. Men who survive the boondocks and make it back to corporate headquarters almost always have taken the trouble to become local anthropologists. When they are transferred or assigned to a small company town they immediately set about the business of learning and adapting to local customs and weaving themselves into the social fabric. You can begin by making a trip to the local library and reading various city documents or back issues of the local newspaper to find out who's who and what interests the people.

If it is a sports-minded town, you can be sure that the top events will be played up on the front page of the daily newspaper. If the town has cultural ambitions, you can be sure that its concert series or its local dramatic society will be prominently mentioned. Once you have an idea as to what the interests of the town are, you can more easily proceed to make yourself a part of the community. If the town is high on Little League action and you become coach of one of the teams that does well, perhaps the company publicist will pump out a release that could somehow find its way to headquarters.

In addition to becoming involved in community affairs, it is imperative that you know the local value system. For example, suppose you have been assigned to a town in Massachusetts that might best be described as a mill town. It relies heavily on its textile factories to provide employment for a large workforce made up predominantly of French-Canadian Catholics and a large colony of second-generation Greeks. Under such circumstances, you should familiarize yourself with various holidays and national heroes. For example, the Greek Easter falls on a different day from that on which Easter is celebrated by most other Christian nationalities. Another example from the same town: The most popular American sport is football. In an Indiana town, however, the major sport would in all likelihood be basketball. This is easily determined—just look at the space assigned each sport in the local newspaper.

How Much Participation?

A word of caution as to community participation—avoid spreading yourself too thin. Keep in mind the company's objectives, find a related local need, and fill it. As Archimedes said: "Give me but one firm spot on which to stand, and I will move the earth."

If you work for an education firm, get involved in school activity. Your job portfolio won't be diminished by your having been on a school board. If your company is in the printing business, you might interest the local library in an exhibit that the appropriate people in your company could help you set up. The attendant publicity would help both you and the company.

Privacy is one of the major problems in relocating to a smaller town. In a large city, a man can get lost in the crowd. Few people know what his activities were the night before, or who his friends are, or his opinions on local issues. Not so in a small town.

A rule that might serve as a general guide for corporate behavior in the boondocks: Never push. Instead, wait for invitations. The invitation may come from a supervisor on the next level or it may come from your boss. Perhaps you will be invited to the local country club. But go only at the superior's invitation.

One of the great levelers in American society is sport. You won't have a chance to rub shoulders with the top man in your corporation at many local events, but you might be able to approach a man on the next level who can help you. Local football, basketball, and baseball games are ideal, especially if you and the man you're trying to cultivate have children of the same age.

When a Bigwig Visits

What if the president or the division boss comes to town? What is the best way to be noticed? Quite frankly, there is no way, unless you are on the path he will travel or at a meeting on his agenda. If you are high enough on the ladder to have him notice positive memos or production charts, that much might be helpful. Anonymity, however, is probably the best approach. A visiting dignitary dislikes seeing junior executives popping in and out of offices like Mexican jumping beans as he walks down the hall to see the general manager or plant foreman. In fact, some eager beavers never quite recover from the withering stares that can come from a superior as he moves quickly to his destination. Most visiting top executives simply do not have time to listen to a junior executive and his problems.

If, however, you do have a chance at a meeting or other gathering, say what you have to say and quickly get off stage. Make your point clearly, succinctly, and reasonably, and don't be petulant or carping about your fellow workers. If there is anything a visiting executive doesn't want to hear it is squabbling, especially among those from whose number he might one day choose his successor. If you do get his ear and have said your piece, don't stand around shuffling your feet waiting to be dismissed. If he begins to talk with someone else, politely excuse yourself. If you've made the right impression, he will remember you.

What if you are in a large city and there is little opportunity to see that your community involvement is brought to the attention of the power brokers in the main office? The most obvious answer in this case is to do a superlative job. It's that little extra effort that can result in home office recognition. By extra effort, I do not mean nervous energy. I mean hard work, which includes taking the time to analyze your mistakes so that you profit by them. Success is often a matter of inches. It's the old story of the young man who has two paper routes instead of one. He could be like everyone else and have one, but he prefers both because of the challenge and the fact that it gives him a leg up. As Donald Kendall, chairman of the board of Pepsico, Inc., has said: "The man who moves up is a 'man in a hurry.'" He has also said, "You can't send a man out to do a job you can't do yourself."

Make one extra call on a client even if you don't "feel" like it. It will pay off. Meet the boys at the bar a little later after work, but put the final touches on the interoffice report. Come in early one morning. It won't disrupt your schedule that much.

Kendall says that the best advice he ever got was a single sentence—"Don't forget to say hello to the man running the elevator." In other words, in all your dealings remain human. Show that you are available and interested in the other person's welfare.

When You Visit the Home Office
Most of the material in this chapter touches a number

of areas that are discussed in greater detail in the chapter relating to attaining a high visibility factor within a company. The major problem with being assigned to an out-of-the-way outpost remains: how to maintain a positive visibility factor with executives at headquarters.

The man who comes from the boondocks to the main office may have an advantage because top executives often feel as though they are not in touch with what is happening "out there." If you do get a chance to visit the main office, having any number of informational tidbits at your disposal will help your cause immeasurably. But be sure you've done your homework. Perhaps your wife or a friend could ask the type of question you are likely to be asked when you arrive.

In addition to being briefed on the specifics of the project that you must take care of while at corporate headquarters, you would do well to have other "marginal" information ready for verbal dissemination.

For example, you may be approached by a division executive who seems very curious about the region where you work. He may appear to be merely curious, but perhaps he knows or has access to information that you are not privy to. Perhaps he is about to be reassigned as your new boss. In other words, don't take any casual questioning too lightly. And be prepared to be helpful—not obsequious—but helpful. An inquisitive higher-up may either be planning a visit, and therefore be looking for information, or be interested in your position and where you work because he is in charge of assigning other subordinates.

It does help to visit the main office, and therefore take advantage of any opportunity to do so. In addition to being seen, you register with potential rivals when you come in on a special mission. It keeps them guessing and makes them more sensitive to your position in the company. A few words on what to do when you arrive at corporate headquarters: Keep your eyes open and the tape recorder in your brain working. Absorb, absorb, absorb.

Broaden Your Base

Do not limit yourself to your particular area of expertise and the people you have come to see. Find out about other areas that interest you. For example, if you are working in a boondocks plant that produces engine parts, perhaps you are interested in the sales department—how the parts are sold once they are produced. The overall sales function usually is coordinated at company headquarters. So take the opportunity to meet people in various sales capacities at headquarters. That way you can learn precisely what the company's sales policy and sales objectives are. You are also adding to your fund of knowledge and broadening your capabilities. As a result, when you return, you may even be able to talk to a superior about being transferred to an area that may offer advancement at a much more rapid rate than the area you are in right now.

If you have no opportunity to chat with other men in different positions in the main office, either because they are unwilling or because it seems as though you are straying from your avowed purpose, you may be able to talk after hours. Before you leave for the main office, send a letter of introduction and perhaps you can gain a brief interview with the man you want to see— even if he's in a different department.

But the main purpose of coming to headquarters is to establish a company presence and gain an opportunity to absorb and broaden your management-knowledge base. If you learn something in the main office about another aspect of the company, it can be put to work when you return.

A man who has been assigned to a far outpost of the corporation must be a good communicator. Not only does he have to make himself understood to those he works and lives with, he must also maintain some sort of communication with the people who count at company headquarters.

One of the prime skills necessary to maintaining a link with the head office is the art of the written report. Above all, it must be clear, concise, and to the point. Often a written report is a subordinate's only means of catching the eye of a superior many miles away.

However, do not restrict your report writing to requests for information from superiors in the home office or memos to your boss. You can and should also write for information from people on the lower echelons at headquarters. For example, suppose you want information on a new production method that seems applicable to your plant. A brief note or detailed memo to a man not necessarily in your department, but who has the information you seek, might be personally profitable to you. He just might show the memo, or mention it in passing, to one of your superiors. Indeed, he himself might one day be your boss—or your subordinate, for that matter. It does not hurt to know one more man in the company. But do not overdo this method of communication. Request only essential information and also be sure that it cannot otherwise be obtained. Nothing exasperates a superior in the main office quite so much as a request for something that can be handled locally.

The Role of Your Wife

One of your major supports, wherever you are assigned, will be your wife. If she is resistant to the
boondocks, it will be doubly hard for you to adjust.
But usually a wife is helpful in adjusting.

There are internal and external roles for the corporate wife. The internal role is as comforter, listener
to your woes, and supporter in what you do. The external role is social, and can help immeasurably, particularly in an out-of-the-way location. If you are in a
job that requires that your wife entertain, she must
be an accomplished hostess and at ease with people.

If you are assigned to a small community, you and
your wife cannot avoid being identified very closely
with your company, so be prepared for a certain loss
of privacy. Even if your wife does not have to take
part in the social whirl as part of business, she can
still cause you problems. One cannot hide a vociferous,
bitter, or argumentative wife in a small town. And
people may conclude that she reflects your values.
If she flouts or takes exception to local customs or attitudes, the community will respond with hostility and
make it harder for you to adjust to its way of life. If
she treads on the feelings of your subordinates or their
wives, it can show up in their work attitudes. As a result, you may well be transferred—but for negative
reasons.

On the other hand, a gregarious and supportive wife
can be of immense help in a small town. If she is an
organizer and is readily available for community projects and school, library, or volunteer work, she is
bound to come into contact with people who can help
you in your present position. In this way, she can
hasten a call to headquarters.

The Positive Uses of the Boondocks

What about establishing a clique or small empire in the boondocks as a way of attracting attention or establishing a power base away from the home office? It is my belief that a good man does not need to build empires. The top executive utilizes a number of good men, but it is not necessary for him to build fierce loyalty in a small group around him.

A lesson may be drawn from other departments that in corporate life have sometimes been referred to as empires. For example, most computer departments are always hunting for new customers in their own company to justify their top-heavy existence. Don't unwillingly become a client for another "profit center." Don't allow your department to be used, and do not use others to get ahead.

Do not worry about whether the bigwigs see what you are doing. If you establish an empire in the territory, they'll see all too soon. The line of reasoning at headquarters when your annual review comes up will then sound like this: "If Jack Jones is setting up his little empire out there in Keokuk, I can imagine what he'll be like if he comes to headquarters." The fact that you have a large number of men working or reporting to you is no guarantee that you'll be promoted faster.

Yet the boondocks can genuinely be a stepping-stone. For one thing, the competition is unlikely to be as vicious as it is at headquarters. For another, you may be able to establish the sort of work relationship with your peers where you can learn much about the company in a leisurely manner. For yet another, you can concentrate on doing a good job on one level while establishing yourself as a man able to adjust and, if need be, troubleshoot. Best of all, you will be under less pressure to produce. If you do produce, then you will reach the powers that be. If you show that you can operate on your own, the men in charge will be disposed to send you to troubled areas, where you will have the opportunity to add to your reputation. So look upon an assignment to the boondocks not as a one-way ticket to oblivion, but as a positive opportunity, keeping in mind that your aim is still to reach the top. It may seem like a circuitous route to an eager-beaver on the way up, but if you master your assignment at the first outpost, you may find that the path has been cleared for a much more rapid and satisfying ascent.

Resist the temptation to isolate yourself in an already isolated atmosphere. That can only be counterproductive. Above all, do not become a passive reactor: continue to learn what you can in preparation for the day you receive the call to the center of power at the main office.

MANAGING TIME
CREATIVELY

8

The most encouraging aspect of the ability to manage time is that it is not an innate ability. Managing time can be learned. In fact, a rather large number of men with less than considerable talent have made careers out of this effectiveness—the most obvious being the mechanical, stereotyped, time-study man.

This chapter is not intended as a rote lesson in effectiveness, but rather as a means for adding a tool to a well-rounded advancement kit. The art of creatively managing time is certain to become more important as the decade progresses because of the strong possibility that the four-day work week will become standard in the corporate world. This chapter will not tell you how to schedule every minute of your executive time between 9:00 A.M. and 5:00 P.M., but instead will focus on some common problems of the overscheduled or underscheduled employee. The emphasis will be on countering the ways that energies are misdirected in nonproductive tasks by suggesting the best channels for routing psychic energy so as to increase productivity. In short, one must be creative with time.

It is not enough to have ability and experience; you must learn how to make effective use of your potential. The secret of managing time is to apply a process of selective inattention to the various tasks that confront you. In other words, one must first determine a goal, and then, setting aside for the moment other tasks and other goals, pursue the most direct means to reach it.

To do this, you must have a system. By system I mean a personal methodology that includes written notes to yourself as well as inner rules and regulations. Your system should also include an internal clock, one that operates on a priority basis. A priority is the item most important to you in achieving your goal at your management level. And the priority in any system should involve people. You will spend a large majority of your time as a manager dealing with people problems. There is no way to anticipate the problems caused by the many varieties of human interaction possible on a job. But if you are aware that people problems come before paper problems, you will then be able to focus on how best to manage your time with subordinates or superiors.

People or Paper Problems?
Don't make the middle management mistake of burrowing into paper problems at the expense of personal involvement. Schedule people in your office at specific times, but be prepared to spend more time in person-to-person meetings than on opening letters or dictating memos to a secretary. No subordinate, much less a superior, likes to be ushered out before his business is

finished. If you set aside a number of free hours during which to casually meet with others, you can help reduce their apprehension about what you may have in mind. An informal invitation to "drop by the office before 10:30" can be quite productive.

When you do schedule an appointment for a specified time and it runs over, set up another appointment right away. Do not abruptly end the interview with a vague "We'll get together again." You don't want the man to leave feeling half satisfied, or that you are so busy you can't spare any more time, or that you meet with others only at your convenience. Make him feel worthy by establishing a new meeting time at the conclusion of the interview.

Once you have established your priorities, you must then add flexibility. How often have you changed your schedule to suit the other party? If you haven't ever done so (except in an emergency), you may be too rigid. Not many top management men feel the need for off time. Consequently they very rarely set time aside for thinking. It is while daydreaming or temporarily relaxing that one is able to make contact with many marginal thoughts and feelings that have been repressed or shunted aside in the hustle and bustle of practical reality. Guilt persists in executives when they are "caught" staring out of a window, apparently daydreaming. Dreaming is a good source of inspiration, and fantasy can be useful. Yet keep such rumination in perspective. As Thomas Edison said: "Genius is one percent inspiration and 99 percent perspiration."

The Trap of Overscheduling

At the other extreme of time management lies the trap of overscheduling. Overscheduling turns executives into clock watchers and robs them of the freedom to work intensely on a particular problem. If a man knows that in ten minutes he has another appointment, it will be almost impossible to maintain his concentration on the present one. Many overschedulers hop from appointment to appointment, avoiding close contact and, in some cases, decisions. The overscheduler is like the whirligig beetle, which circles about rapidly on the surface of still water. And his circles, like those of the whirligig, rarely go beneath the surface.

So be sure there is some leeway in your schedule. Leave yourself extra time to go from one appointment to another. With that extra time, think about the discussion you've just had and then mentally prepare for the next appointment. Don't become a dynamo giving off more heat than productive energy.

Another way to curb a tendency to overschedule is to delegate authority. For example, if you are a $20,000 a year man, you should not be moving office furniture. This doesn't apply, of course, to helping a secretary move a typewriter. But, in addition to making people who should be charged with moving furniture uncomfortable with your presence, you tarnish the image of an authority figure. You may think you are being democratic, but you are probably just avoiding another task more relevant to your position. In fact, you could be undermining morale by interfering with a chore best negotiated on a lower level.

The man who is overscheduled is usually a compulsive type who must maintain control. The higher you climb in a company, the less interfering you must become. Overscheduling can be alleviated by giving up control of all detail work. No man who is running a department or section likes to have the president of the company butt in to suggest why he should hire a new junior man. If your assistant sales manager wants to hire a secretary to conform to his specifications, let him. Don't impose your attitudes on him because it makes you more comfortable to do so.

Get Out of the Office

Part of your free-thinking time should be spent out of your office. This is another area usually glossed over by management studies. Management consultants all recognize that a man should have outside interests as alternative satisfactions, but few advocate free time on company time as a method for adding to peak efficiency. Not leaving your office to go out for lunch can, over a period of time, be harmful. One needs to break routine. Even while you're at a social lunch, thoughts are still percolating in your head, and if you avoid a three-martini supplement, you often come back to the office raring to go. So recognize the positive function of a lunch break. Even a walk to another part of the building can furnish a fresh perspective.

Whenever possible, attend industry functions. They can serve the same general purpose. Attending relevant industry and trade association meetings can be a good way to generate ideas. True, many such meetings are a waste of time and effort, but even a brief boondoggle trip can be refreshing. I suspect that many top executives disparage the practice of attending out-of-town meetings because they do not want their middle managers to be exposed to rival companies.

The parochial manager with little life experience always finds it difficult moving to a higher level. Industry meetings are fine opportunities to broaden your base. They put you in contact with new men with new ideas, ideas that can be translated into programs of your own when you return to your office.

The Pitfall of Underachievement

The parochial middle manager usually exhibits signs of what the psychology profession labels "underachieving." Underachievers are those who usually never quite produce what superiors know they can. As in many psychiatric disorders, the underachiever maintains a self-image that tells him that he cannot add experience. He then uses this self-image to support his conviction that he is stupid or inept. So he is often an enigma to top executives, who know that he can do a job and are puzzled as to why he doesn't. One of the underachiever's dominant characteristics is that he wastes time. He is an expert at postponing a chore, no matter how urgent. Such behavior indicates a man who, for some psychological reason, is sabotaging his own efforts to advance. Most wasted time is wasted in performing the easy chores. The time waster constantly repeats already mastered tasks unnecessarily because he feels more comfortable doing so. It's like a newly purchased pair of shoes. You really like them and immediately start wearing them. But they pinch, and will of course continue to until your feet become accustomed to them, and so you return to a pair of battered, but comfortable, shoes. It's a mistake to put off a challenge because it is new or difficult. With perseverance both hard and easy tasks will become standardized, just as new shoes eventually become comfortable.

Tackle the Toughest Chore

If you keep a checklist of chores and you persist in putting off a particular item week after week, chances are you are avoiding a priority. One way to tell the

119

importance of a chore is by the amount of tenseness it causes in you and the degree of avoidance involved.

Test yourself. You are sitting in the office with your two-day-old list of chores in front of you. The first three items are letters to out-of-town destinations; the fourth is a memo to your boss. The fifth, sixth, and seventh tasks pertain to lateral relationships in the office. Instead of doing the easy chores—the letters and speaking to your peers—concentrate on No. 4— the memo to the boss, the one chore that makes you tense. Work to erase it from the list immediately. That way you will ease the pressure on the other six items.

If you find that the tension builds to a point where it can no longer be ignored, or alleviated, or momentarily checked by doing something else, that is a signal to begin the avoided task. Tenseness usually reaches a peak and can be ended only by a direct approach to the feared task.

Try to tackle the toughest chore first thing in the morning. Eventually the "toughies" will be almost routine. But if you wait until midafternoon or four-thirty to work on the toughest job of all, it is easy to say: "Well, I'll get around to that one tomorrow. No harm in putting it off one more day since there's no deadline on it."

Another method of solving tough tasks is to determine what your peak-efficiency work period is. Most people operate on an energy timetable, and schedules are a highly personal matter. There are people who stay up late at night watching movies or talk shows; there are those who retire in the early evening and then wake up early raring to go. So it is in the office. Often a man can do his best work in the morning. I once had a boss who liked to call this person an "A" type, the real get-up-and-go type, who begins to run out of creative juice somewhere around one o'clock in the afternoon. Then there are what he dubbed "B" types. They rev up very slowly after morning coffee, shift into high gear after lunch, and then zoom past five at peak efficiency levels. Whatever your inner schedule, it is best to cope with the most nettlesome problems during peak efficiency periods because, in addition to having increased mental capacity, you will probably dispense with the task faster—thus saving time.

Avoid Job Drift

For what it is worth, here is a schedule plan that I found helpful in my own work. I always kept a small list with numbered items. At the end of the day, I would review my little list to see what I had finished (always crossing off a chore as I completed it). I would then compile my list for the next day, moving up to the No. 1 spot any important chore that I had neglected to do. Then I would list in order of importance the other chores. I would leave the list in a prominent place on my desk, and when I came to work the next morning, immediately set about the first order of business—usually after opening my mail and taking care of unexpected business. If I found myself avoiding a particular chore, I would circle and underline it to make sure that I got to it without further dillydallying. By reviewing the list at the end of the day, I could plan for the next day, and also help reinforce decisions and transactions of that particular day.

In addition, every two or three months, I would check a self-imposed job description to see if I was fulfilling all the criteria I had set for myself. If you are in a company that issues job descriptions, you can check to make sure that your time is geared to fulfilling your own. Although job descriptions are always written for "the other guy" and not yourself, and are usually obsolete before they are circulated (everyone should consider his job as evolutionary), there are still some instances where checking can assist planning. It curbs job drift.

Overachieve in Managing Your Time

The man who manages time most effectively is the overachiever. He usually has less native ability than the underachiever, but he knows his goals and works hard to reach them. Often he is a plodder. There is an analogy, obviously, with the tale of the tortoise and the hare.

Psychologists point out that the same dynamic can account for both the underachiever and the overachiever behavior patterns. Both may be men with low self-esteem, but where the underachiever gives up and succumbs to his own despairing self-image, the overachiever covers his low self-esteem with grim determination. He labors to prove that he is as capable as the next man, and though his underlying lack of self-confidence shows occasionally, he develops a cover that serves him well. Many overachievers need, and constantly seek, the approval of some type of authority figure. Often, if they don't get that approval, they plunge in and "get lost" in their work. The important aspect, however, is that they complete their work and are able to outdistance many rivals by sheer drive.

The trick to managing time effectively is to build in overachievement capabilities while maintaining a sense of satisfaction from doing a job well. Because many overachievers must constantly appease the almost insatiable demands of their low self-esteem, or constantly prove to peers that they are as good as anyone else, they fail to experience achieved goals as satisfying.

At the end of the day it is pleasant to look over your little list and note that you have accomplished what you set out to do. By doing that, one makes it possible to add more responsibilities—a fact of life in the upper reaches of management. Consider it a sin to waste time.

If you are a man who derives satisfaction from well-planned office time you will then better be able to enjoy yourself outside business. There will be fewer occasions when unfinished work interferes with social projects.

Also, squeeze more business activity into your off hours. You may run over the day's possibilities as you sit in that commuter train or in your car on the way to work. In that way you start your personal dynamo before you reach the office. If you drive to work, you can set down your thoughts on a tape recorder (if you have one), just as you can always carry a small notebook for the same purpose. As noted before, you can use your lunch hour for getting a fresh approach to some chore.

Never discount the potential value of free time. If, at some point after embarking on the day's chores, you sense that you aren't going to accomplish as much as you would like, set up "minigoals." Dismantle a large problem so that it is more manageable. A complicated memo, for example, does not have to be written at one sitting. Outlining it or breaking it down into its components and dealing with one component a day may be helpful. By the end of the week you will have five major components of one memo ready to assemble. When a particular task on your schedule seems insurmountable, talk it over with a colleague.

Occasionally, nothing goes right. When that happens it is probably best not to push. If politics is the art of the possible, so is managing time effectively. Yet keep in mind its principal requirements: a flexible schedule, an awareness of your own energy cycle, an emphasis on human-centered goals, and a willingness to overcome a fear of difficult tasks.

CLIMBING
THE MONETARY LADDER   9

Do you know what your fellow executives are paid?
How many times have you openly compared paychecks
with a friend in the office to see what has been deducted
by that *bête noir*, the federal government? How often
do you wonder how your office mates can afford to live
so well?

Managers can hardly be blamed for their curiosity
in a corporate structure that places a premium on salary secrecy. But it is not difficult to understand why
salaries are top secret in most corporations (as compared with salaries in public service). Secrecy reflects
management's desire to deflect the focus away from
real inequities in its system of monetary reward. Would
that secretiveness were not a fact of corporate life.

Consequently, raises are rarely sought directly for
their own sake, but for a completed or well-performed
task, or because "baby needs new shoes"—anything
but the real reason. Is it possible to imagine a man

saying to his boss that he needs a raise to buy a new swimming pool? That type of request is simply not in the canon of acceptable wants and needs as promulgated by the business ethic. A man needs a raise because of reasons that are acceptable to the corporation and that fit the corporation's rationale of why he should receive a raise. Acceptable items on the raise roster are children, school, housing. Very rarely are "frivolities," such as extended vacations and time off to spend with one's children, accepted as valid reasons.

Avoid Irrational Loyalty

As top management holds to its preconceived notions of the proper use of raises, so do their middle managers cling to the myth of loyalty to a company. Some middle managers persist in assuming that pledges of loyalty to a company will result in proper and automatic raises. They persevere in the myth that the company will "take care of them," and end by avoiding responsibility for their own movement. Although younger men entering the business ranks are job-hopping with greater frequency and discovering that mobility does pay off, the majority of middle management executives still do not dare show such "disloyalty." Irrational loyalty abounds in business. And for all the palaver about upward mobility and frequent moves, job-switching is still not widely practiced—even though a conclusive number of studies show that the most successful men are those who do change jobs often.

Irrational loyalty flourishes among the insecure, and since the attachment to security increases as one ages, security becomes a sort of armor that executives wrap themselves in. The corporation is quite capable of using a man's irrational loyalty to keep him within its orbit. If a company knows that a man is afraid to reassess his course in the business world, it has a powerful tool, especially when it is euphemistically labeled loyalty.

Another illustration: There are many second-in-commands who do not recognize that the man to whom they have attached themselves is in the process of losing his job or is being passed over. Rather than accelerate to a new position, the right-hand man ignores what is happening and becomes paralyzed just at the point when he should be most active.

Do not be seduced by a company's or a boss's flattering references to your loyalty. If you have assessed your position and feel you deserve a raise or promotion, do not hesitate to ask because it would seem disloyal.

The Mobility Factor
In the early 1960s, established management raised a great hue and cry over the new-breed executive—who was quickly labeled a job-hopper. At that time, job-switching aroused fear in many older management men that they could no longer count on company loyalty among the young executives as a way to keep them. Now, in the seventies, the mobile manager is accepted, and most astute management men agree that it is essential for a man to learn to move once or twice before making a final commitment to a company (even though most still linger on one job too long).

There are many advantages for current middle managers because of the precedents set by the mobile managers of the sixties, including faster promotions. The way has also been eased for the young executives of the 1970s. As George F. James, former dean of the

Columbia University Graduate School of Business and an ex–senior vice-president at Mobil Oil Corporation, has wryly expressed it: "Lacking experience, they don't know a lot of things that aren't true." And even though the convenient tag of an opportunistic and not-loyal company man is sometimes still attached to an exiting man, it is not taken as seriously as in the past. For one thing, your superior would be hesitant to so label you if you left the company for another job because he himself probably came to the company from another job. However, change for its own sake does not lead to the corporate heights.

Getting Your Raise: Think Before You Ask

Before you hit the appropriate gentleman for a raise, some personal homework needs doing. For example, do you have rapport with the man you must ask? Have you planted the optimum "situation" in his mind?

Establishing rapport with your boss is discussed elsewhere, but the best way to plant a positive situation is by seeing to it that some personal project of yours is either moving well or has been successfully concluded. When this is the case, alert your superior, making certain that he is well aware that the project went well or is going well for the company, for him, and for yourself. If possible, use figures and sales charts to document your success.

All requests for raises should be broached only after you have mentally answered all possible surprises that a superior may spring in an effort to postpone or squelch your request. Do not be involved with any bogged-down projects when you "pitch" your superior. Make sure that orders in all recent memos that he has sent you have been carried out, or at the very least, discussed with him to *his* apparent satisfaction. Do not leave any loose ends for him to seize.

Remember the cardinal rule of getting a raise: Don't wait for the company to approach you. If you do, you will inevitably be offered less than you think you deserve. In fact, beware the shrewd boss who realizes that you are itching for a raise and anticipates you by offering a lesser pay hike. If this occurs, hold your anger in check. State very simply that you had planned to come to him about a raise and are very pleased and gratified that he anticipated your need and approached you first. However, upon thinking about his offer, you have decided that it doesn't quite measure up to what you had in mind. You wondered: Is there any basis for further discussion? By stating in a friendly manner that an offer is inadequate, you leave your boss the option of coming back with a better offer. Both of you are then in a position to reach a satisfactory compromise.

Part of your preparations for requesting a raise should include familiarizing yourself with the pay scale in your company. Pay scales in various industries differ widely. For example, newspaper and publishing personnel are notoriously low paid when compared with sales personnel. So if you can determine how much the president of a company makes (you might check the annual reports for information), or, if possible, how much your immediate boss earns, you will then have some idea of the scale in your company. The pay for top executives usually follows a closely-patterned structure. Thus if you know what the president or a man near the top makes, you can guess what the salary level is where you are.

Salary scales in a public company are obviously more "out front" than they are in a privately owned firm.

It is possible, however, to estimate structures in tight-lipped industries. In industries where men stay at the same level for many years (utilities, railroads, and so forth), accumulating automatic raises, the problem can be nettlesome, but it is still possible to determine what a company's pay scale is.

Remember: A low salary in one field or company is often considered a fairly high salary in another. An American Management Association figure on executive compensation may serve as a rough guidepost for pay patterns. In a $100 million company, if the president were making $100,000, the No. 2 man would usually get 70 percent as much, or $70,000. The No. 3 man would probably get 60 percent of the president's pay, the No. 4 man 50 percent, and so on down the line. If you find that your president makes $50,000, then readjust the figures accordingly.

The Benefits for You

Once you reach the $25,000–$35,000 bracket, extras will be "laid on" you. In the last half of the 1960s, extra incentives reached new and ingenious limits, with a wide variety of stock options and bonuses offered. One reason executive compensation is so inventive is that the men who think of benefits are usually the recipients. Some benefits, while seemingly trivial, have a meaning all their own. We have heard repeatedly about the significance of a windowed office, a corner office, an office with a rug. Then, too, it's original paintings for top level executives, copies and prints for middle management.

But the top executive payroll is not where you are at present. Often the man to whom you speak about a raise has forgotten how to identify with your position in the chain of command. In other words, your needs at this point in time do not coincide with his. Therefore, you must communicate the necessity for cash (inflation has eaten away most of your paycheck, and so forth). He will surely be aware of inflation even if he has been able to combat it with his various other methods of compensation (stock options, for one). So when you make your approach, keep in mind that you must get your point across. Do not become involved with trying to talk to him on his status level, but do try to mention common monetary concerns. Don't talk about his plane, talk about a barbecue in the backyard. You must convince him that money is indeed important to you (at this point in your career), and so tell him, if necessary, that someday you may be in his position, but that right now you need the cash for a host of goods.

Is It Dangerous to Ask?

How do you know when to ask for a raise? When you feel that you deserve one because a project has been successfully completed that was very important to the company (no matter how little time it took), when you know the company policy is for an almost automatic raise every six months, when you have convinced your superior that you are indispensable to the department.

Many people hesitate to ask for a raise for fear of being turned down. The real fear is not a fear of being rejected, it is the dread of making a decision about one's future course. For once you are turned down, the inevitable thought emerges: Should I leave the company? Remember what Thomas Jefferson once said, "The merchant has no country."

And don't fret over being fired for "pushiness" or disagreement with company policy. There is a famous story about one "Max-a-billion" Palevsky. In the early 1960s, Palevsky was fired as a vice-president of a Packard Bell computer division when he disagreed on company goals. At the time, this latter day Horatio Alger hero was making $30,000 a year. He then borrowed close to $1 million and started his own firm, which he called Scientific Data Systems. By 1969, Palevsky was a major factor in a $940 million merger with Xerox. As Palevsky says, "Being fired can be wonderful." Although it is not often mentioned, a firing can help a career because it forces you to redefine goals, figure out what went wrong, and decide what you must do in the future.

Contrary to what most middle managers believe, asking for a raise can be a way to impress a superior. The manner in which you ask for a raise and the way you present it can make a positive impression, so do not always assume that you must appear hat in hand to seek alms from an omnipotent authority figure. If a top executive sees that you have the mettle to confront him with your ability, he will then think about your positive qualifications for functioning on a higher level.

Among the qualities you put on display when you ask for a raise: company loyalty, self-confidence (which must not manifest itself as brashness), belief in your own ideas, and above all, that little extra that separates the top executive from the middle management pack— drive. A subordinate who persuades a superior to give him a raise builds appreciation and respect among the top executive echelon, and probably to a greater degree than he ever thought possible. Think of your own experience. How did you feel when a subordinate came to you for a raise? Think back and I am sure you'll recall that most of the men who approached you had marshaled their facts and were indeed deserving. In time you probably admired them for blowing their own horn—provided, of course, they were not obnoxious about it. Of course, there are the something-for-nothing types, but most people have a built-in barometer, and know when they are deserving of a raise. For the most part, they are right.

Never procrastinate about asking for a raise. For one thing, dawdling just builds up stress and tends to affect your work and your relationship with your boss. Most men who emerge from the boss's office after having asked for a raise feel relieved—even if they've been turned down. At the very least, the boss now knows how the man feels.

Expect a Counter Move

Suppose, after you have screwed up your courage and popped the question, the boss smilingly says: "Well, John, because of our cash position and sales picture this year, we cannot give you a raise at this time. However, we can offer you a new position which should be quite challenging for you and if you work out in it, we can then talk about a raise. As it stands now, at your present job level I can't give you any more money." What is your response? On the face of it, it sounds very flattering to be offered a new position. However, when you arrive home that night and tell your wife that you have not gotten a raise, she probably will have a hard time understanding just how the company has your best interests in mind. She was counting on that raise for a new dishwasher and you were planning to use it to help pay for the new car.

When a boss surprises you with a counter move (in lieu of money), one of the best reactions is to put his proposal in a "holding pattern." In other words, tell him you are pleased with the thought of a new and challenging position, but were not prepared to hear him offer one. You came in expressly to discuss what you consider a well-deserved raise, but now that he has introduced a new element you would like to go home and think about it for a day or two. At the same time, closely question him as to just what the new position is and what your responsibilities would be—and try to commit him to a definite date for a raise on the *new* job. Also, try to determine whether he would object if you stayed on your present assignment.

Once you have found out exactly what the new job entails, it may be to your advantage to take it even if there is no immediate pay hike. It may offer you an opportunity to broaden your base and learn some skills that can help you later in your career. Unwittingly, your superior may have helped make it possible for you to gain valuable work experience at a critical stage.

Choose the Right Moment

Picking the precise time to seek an increase can be a delicate matter. Be sure to have your antenna tuned to detect any slight discomfort or negative mood in your boss. For example, do not approach him when he is overwhelmed with paperwork or a duty he must perform immediately. You might be able to lay the groundwork on a company trip or trade association meeting where, in a relaxed atmosphere, over drinks or around the swimming pool, you may be able to let him know that you have some pressing financial need. After establishing this, and not asking for a raise directly, you can approach him more formally in his office when you return from your trip. If you have made a well-received presentation at the meeting, the juxtaposition of your hint that you might need a raise with the positive response to your presentation will not be lost on him.

But beware: If you ask for a raise at an inopportune time and are turned down, you may irreparably damage your reputation in the company. The shrewd raise-getter knows that he is 90 percent sure of obtaining a raise when he applies. If, after examining your case very carefully to make certain that you can answer any possible objections, you still have doubts, postpone and rework your presentation.

The Other Job Offer

Should another job offer be employed as a tactic for gaining a raise? Only if you are sure that when you say that you have been offered another job elsewhere, you are prepared to leave. This applies even if you do not in fact have a firm offer. One of the advantages to having another job offer is psychological. Not only will you feel more assured when you ask for a raise, but your boss will be impressed with the fact that another company wants you. You automatically become more desirable—even if it is only to keep you from the competition.

Caution: Do not bang your superior over the head with a job offer. It is best to play it down while making your point. You might say: "I'm in a terrible bind, John, and I just don't know what to do. Therefore, I've come to you for your advice on this matter." After that sort of opening statement, you tell him that you've been approached by another firm with an offer that seems hard to turn down. Naturally, you came to him to get his help in assessing your future with the company and perhaps his thoughts on what you should do. In this way, you have not made any commitment. If he asks about the position offered you, tell him about it in general terms. He is probably curious to see what counter offer he will have to make in order to keep you. You do not have to name the company, but you certainly can tell him that you will have increased responsibility, more money, and so forth. Do not present the new opportunity as an accomplished fact. Give the man a chance to come back with a counter offer. Nothing can bring a raise faster than the threat of moving to another company—provided your present company thinks highly of you. In other words, your boss must be able to justify a raise for you to *his* boss on the grounds that the company would otherwise lose a good man.

If he says that a raise is ''out of the question'' and he sounds as though you should take the other job, he may be informing you that your future with your present company is limited. In a way he is doing you a favor by confirming what you probably have not wanted to face yourself.

A final word about climbing the monetary ladder. Reliance on the corporation or your immediate superior as the beneficent and thoughtful authority figure who will reward you for your service to the company is a head-in-the-sand approach. Of course, there are a few enlightened superiors in the business world, but the majority of executives are not eager to part with company cash. Don't count on the fact that your boss will ''notice'' you. Ascension to the board room can be slowed immeasurably by a wait and see attitude.

The future belongs to those who take it. You should be no exception. If you are to be the bright young man in a company there is no reason why you should not be paid for it. As Benjamin Franklin put it: ''The cat in gloves catches no mice.''